USAF Southeast Asia Monograph Series
Volume VII
Monograph 9

Air Force Heroes in Vietnam

Major Donald K. Schneider

New Imprint by
OFFICE OF AIR FORCE HISTORY
UNITED STATES AIR FORCE
WASHINGTON, D.C., 1985

Library of Congress Cataloging-in-Publication Data

Schneider, Donald K.
Air Force heroes in Vietnam.

(USAF Southeast Asia monograph series; v. 7, monograph 9)
Reprint. Originally published: Maxwell Air Force Base, Ala.: Air University, Air War College; Washington, D.C.: For sale by the Supt. of Docs., U.S. G.P.O., 1979.
Includes index.
1. Vietnamese Conflict, 1961–1975—Aerial operations, American. 2. United States. Air Force—History—Vietnamese Conflict, 1961–1975. 3. Medal of Honor. I. Title. II. Series.
[DS558.8.S36 1986] 959.704'348 85–18908
ISBN 0–912799–32–3

This volume is a reprint of a 1976 edition originally issued by the Air University.

For sale by the Superintendent of Documents, U.S. Government Printing Office
Washington, D.C., 20402

Foreword

This ninth essay of the Southeast Asia Monograph Series tells the stories of the 12 Air Force heroes who were awarded the Congressional Medal of Honor for action in Vietnam. The author, Major Schneider, has chosen a most unusual and effective way of presenting his material, for he is greatly concerned with the contextual aspects of what he describes; that is, he devotes considerable attention to the history of the Medal itself, particularly insofar as airmen of earlier wars are concerned, to the aircraft in which these latest recipients flew, and to the missions with which both the men and their machines were entrusted.

These factors, then, are put in the context of the battle arena—Vietnam, with all of its special conditions and limitations. There 12 airmen of the United States Air Force acted with such courage, devotion, and utter selflessness that they were subsequently awarded the highest recognition that their country could bestow, the Medal of Honor. Three of the men died in the actions for which they were cited. But in one sense at least they and the others will never die, for their actions have insured that their names will live as long as determination, fidelity, bravery, and nobility of spirit are traits that human beings admire.

DAVID L. GRAY, Major General, USAF
Commandant, Air War College

Preface

"I would rather have this medal than be President of the United States." So spoke President Harry S. Truman during a Medal of Honor presentation ceremony at the White House. This sentiment has been shared by soldiers, sailors, and airmen since 1862, when President Lincoln approved an Act of Congress authorizing "medals of honor." A single word etched on the medal's face tells its meaning. The word? VALOR.

Former Air Force Chief of Staff General John D. Ryan describes the stringent requirements for earning the nation's highest military award:

> A member of the American Armed Forces can merit the Medal of Honor in only one manner: by a deed of personal bravery or self-sacrifice, above and beyond the call of duty, while in combat with an enemy of the nation. The gallantry must be certified by two eye-witnesses, and be clearly beyond the call of duty. Moreover, it must involve the risk of life and must be the type of deed that, if not performed, would evoke no criticism of the individual.

This book tells the story of the 12 United States Air Force airmen who won the Medal of Honor in Vietnam from 1966 through 1973. These 12 men are the latest in a line of 60 Air Force heroes whose story began in the skies over France in 1918.

Four airmen won the Medal during World War I. Three were killed in action as a result of their disregard for personal danger. The sole survivor, First Lieutenant Eddie V. Rickenbacker, later became the leading American ace of the war, destroying 26 enemy aircraft by Armistice Day in 1918.

Except for a rare special award, the Medal is given only for gallantry in combat. In 1927, Charles A. Lindbergh was awarded a special Medal of Honor in peacetime for his nonstop flight from New York to Paris in the *Spirit of St. Louis*.

The saga began again in the skies over the Pacific and Japan when Lieutenant Colonel James H. Doolittle became the first Army Air Forces recipient of World War II just four months after the Japanese attack on Pearl Harbor. With the apparent certainty of being forced to land in enemy territory or of perishing at sea, he led a squadron of B–25s in a bombing raid on the Japanese mainland. Thirty-seven airmen joined Doolittle as WW II Medal of Honor winners before the final allied victory in 1945. Of the 38 heroes, 22 were killed in action. On one historic day, the first of August 1943, five pilots earned the Medal during the daring low-level attack on the vast, heavily-defended oil refineries at Ploesti, Rumania. Five heroes were aces, including Major Richard I. Bong, who racked up 40 victories, and Major William A. Shomo, who downed seven Japanese aircraft in one dogfight over the Philippine Islands. Sergeant Maynard H. Smith, serving as a gunner aboard a heavy bomber, became the first enlisted airman to win the nation's highest decoration. On a mission over Europe, his aircraft was hit by enemy fighters and antiaircraft artillery, igniting intense fires in the waist section and radio compartment. Sergeant Smith, single-handedly, gave first aid to the wounded tail gunner, fired the waist guns to ward off opposing fighters, and extinguished the flames.

In the post-war period another special peacetime Medal was awarded posthumously to Brigadier General William Mitchell. He was recognized by Congress in 1946 for outstanding pioneer service and foresight in the field of military aviation. In 1947, the United States Air Force became a separate service, fulfilling one of Billy Mitchell's great dreams.

During the Korean War, fast and maneuverable jet aircraft helped US pilots sweep the skies before the cease-fire in 1953. Three of the four heroes, including Major George A. Davis, a World War II ace who downed 14 enemy aircraft over Korea before winning the Medal, were fighter pilots. The four awards were presented posthumously—each man had made the ultimate sacrifice.

The year is 1966. A small outpost in the jungle is under attack by an overwhelming hostile force while overhead Air Force attack aircraft fight desperately to stave off the enemy. The setting is Southeast Asia, and the scene is set for the personal bravery of Major Bernard F. Fisher, the first Medal of Honor winner in Vietnam. Eleven airmen joined Major Fisher as USAF Medal of Honor winners in the Vietnam conflict. The nature of the air war, which saw the employment of both the most modern aircraft and the unsophisticated machines of World War II vintage, placed unique demands on their courage and initiative. Two heroes are described in each of six chapters dealing with the A–1 Skyraiders, the Forward Air Controllers, the F–105 Wild Weasels, the Helicopters, the Cargo/Gunships, and the Prisoners of War. Three of the twelve men gave their lives. Two were recognized for their heroism in captivity, and one survived 100 missions over the heavily defended north. Others were assigned to combat duty for a year, flying from bases in South Vietnam and Thailand.

Unlike his counterpart in World War II, the American airman in Vietnam was sometimes frustrated by an elusive enemy, restrictions on targets and tactics, and growing discontent on the homefront. But his dedication never wavered. Despite the obstacles, he did the job and did it professionally.

This latest chapter in the saga of men and the flying machines that began in 1918 ended in 1976 when President Ford awarded the Medal to two former prisoners of war. Colonel George E. Day and Captain Lance P. Sijan were the last of twelve Air Force men to win the Medal in Vietnam. They became the 59th and 60th airmen in the gallant line that began with Second Lieutenant Frank Luke, Jr.

" ... TO ALL WHO SERVED "

Acknowledgments

The facilities at Maxwell AFB, Alabama, offer a rich variety of source materials for the study of airpower in Southeast Asia. I am grateful to Mr. Robert B. Lane and his staff at the Air University Library, as well as Mr. Lloyd H. Cornett, Jr. and his staff at the Albert F. Simpson Historical Research Center. I should also like to thank Lieutenant Colonel Gordon F. Nelson, Nonresident Programs Directorate, Air Command and Staff College, who reviewed and edited the manuscript.

The author is also indebted to Ed Blair, Major John T. Correll, Captain Gary A. Guimond, Major Jimmy W. Kilbourne, Robert K. Ruhl, and T. R. Sturm, whose articles appear in *Airman,* and to Flint Du Pre and Laurence W. Zoeller, who have written for *Air Force Magazine*.

CONTENTS

Illustrations

Maps (Action Locations)

AIR FORCE HEROES IN VIETNAM

by

Donald K. Schneider, Major, USAF

Chapter I. The A–1 Skyraiders

The Job

The A–1 Skyraider was well-suited for several combat jobs in Vietnam, flying rescue, close air support, and forward air control (FAC) missions.

In the rescue role the Skyraider pilot was required to locate the downed airman and protect him with the A–1's firepower. He became the on-scene commander of the recovery effort, controlling fighter-bomber strikes on hostile positions and escorting the helicopters during the pickup of the survivor.

On a close air support mission, the Skyraider pilot's ability to attack ground targets with pinpoint precision made the A–1 an outstanding weapon to support friendly troops in contact with the enemy.

In the FAC role, the A–1 pilot was an aerial observer and controller. In constant radio contact with Army units in his sector, he warned of enemy ambushes and then controlled fast-moving fighters in strikes on the hostile positions.

The airman downed deep in enemy territory and the embattled foot soldier caught in a Vietcong (VC) crossfire often depended on the Skyraiders for their very lives.

The Aircraft

The Douglas-built A–1 was a single-engine, propeller-driven, fighter bomber that first saw service with the Navy in World War II. The A–1H was the single-seat model, while the two-seat version was the A–1E.

Though the Skyraider could reach a speed of 400 miles per hour in a dive, it was slow in comparison with the jet fighters. Its slow speed made the A–1 more vulnerable to groundfire, but also gave the pilot more time to find the enemy's concealed positions. Furthermore, the A–1's maneuverability allowed the pilot to make many firing passes on

A–1 Aircraft

the target in rapid succession; it could be quickly turned and repositioned for another attack without leaving the immediate area.

A–1s came to Vietnam in the summer of 1964 and became the workhorses of the Vietnamese Air Force and the mainstay of US Air Force counterinsurgency operations. Eight thousand pounds of ordnance could be hung from its wings, and long endurance (in excess of four hours) made it an ideal aircraft for rescue escort, close air support, or FAC missions. Able to fly in poor weather, withstand small arms and automatic weapons fire, and carry a great variety of ordnance, the Skyraider was a favorite with fighter pilots and FACs.

The Men

Born in 1927, Bernard F. Fisher served briefly in the Navy at the end of World War II and in the Air National Guard from 1947 to 1950. The Idaho native began Air Force officer training in 1951.

Before his assignment to Vietnam, he spent his entire Air Force career as a jet fighter pilot in the Air Defense Command. While stationed at Homestead Air Force Base, Florida, Major Fisher was recognized twice as a result of his landing F–104 Starfighters after a complete failure of the engine oil system. On each occasion he was able to save the crippled craft when ejection would have been the safest course of action.

In 1965 Bernie Fisher volunteered for duty in Vietnam and traded

Maj. Bernard F. Fisher

Lt. Col. William A. Jones III

his fast-moving jet for the venerable Skyraider. As a member of the 1st Air Commando Squadron, he flew 200 combat sorties from July 1965 to June 1966. In addition to the Medal of Honor, Major Fisher earned the Silver Star, the Distinguished Flying Cross and the Air Medal with six oak leaf clusters.

****

Born in 1922, William A. Jones III graduated from the University of Virginia in 1942. He attended the US Military Academy at West Point, graduating in 1945.

Colonel Jones won his wings in 1945 and flew with the Strategic Air Command and a Troop Carrier Wing, with overseas duty in both the Phillipine Islands and Europe.

Before the Medal of Honor mission in 1968, Colonel Jones flew 98 combat missions from Thailand.

In November 1969, William A. Jones III was killed in a private airplane crash at Woodbridge, Virginia.

March 10, 1966

On the 10th of March 1966, Major Bernard F. Fisher and his wingman, Captain Francisco (Paco) Vazquez, took off from Pleiku Air Base in South Vietnam's central highlands.

One hundred and fifty miles to the north, near the Laotian border, lay the Special Forces camp in the A Shau valley. Twenty American Special Forces troops and 375 South Vietnamese soldiers were under attack by over 2,000 North Vietnamese Army Regulars. The siege was in its second day, and the defenders, who had been forced into a single bunker in the northern corner of the outpost, depended on American airstrikes to slow the enemy advance.

The North Vietnamese ringed the valley floor with more than 20 antiaircraft artillery pieces and hundreds of automatic weapons, making it a deadly flak trap for the slow-moving A–1Es. One pilot described it as "like flying inside Yankee Stadium with the people in the bleachers firing at you with machine guns."

Major Fisher and Captain Vazquez joined four other A–1Es orbiting high above A Shau. The pilots were stymied by a deck of low clouds hanging over the valley. Major Fisher had flown here the day before in bad weather, and if there was a way to get down through the murk, he would find it. His luck held: as Bernie located a small hole in the undercast and led the formation of six Skyraiders down towards the jungle floor.

The A–1Es broke into the clear to find that the ragged cloud ceiling lay only 800 feet above the trees, obscuring the tops of the surrounding hills. They would be forced to operate at low altitude, constantly in the sights of the enemy gunners. The Skyraider pilots had nicknamed the narrow valley "the tube" because it was less than a mile wide and six miles long, and provided little maneuvering room for the bombing and strafing runs against the Vietcong.

Restricted by the weather and high terrain, the A–1Es could attack from just one direction. The pilots would be forced to fly straight down the valley, deliver their ordnance during a hard left turn, continue the turn into a tight 180° escape maneuver and race back up the valley. They knew that the North Vietnamese would fill the approach to the valley with a deadly curtain of groundfire.

Bernie Fisher led a string of four Skyraiders on the first pass down the tube while an Army radioman described the hostile positions along the valley's south wall. The enemy gunners found the range, shattering the canopy of Captain Hubert King's aircraft with an accurate burst. No longer able to see out of the bullet-riddled windscreen and having missed death by inches, King pulled out of the fight and headed for Pleiku.

After attacking and escaping successfully, Bernie and the two remaining wingmen immediately hurtled back down the valley on a second strafing pass. Major Dafford W. (Jump) Myers felt his machine lurch. Jump remembered, "I've been hit by 50 calibers before, but this was something bigger, maybe the Chinese 37-millimeter cannon. Almost immediately the engine started sputtering and cutting out, and then it conked out for good. The cockpit filled with smoke. I got on the radio and gave my call sign, Surf 41, and said, 'I've been hit and hit hard.' Hobo 51—that was Bernie—came right back and said, 'Rog, you're on fire and burning clear back past your tail.' I was way too low to bail out so I told him I would have to put it down on the strip."

Though the airstrip was controlled by the enemy and flanked by heavy guns, Jump Myers had no choice as he began a gliding turn toward the touchdown point. His forward vision was blocked by smoke and flame, so Bernie Fisher "talked" him into a proper alignment and rate of descent. As the crippled Skyraider crossed the landing threshold, Major Fisher realized that it was going too fast to stop on the short strip. Bernie warned him to raise the landing gear, and Jump retracted the wheels just before the aircraft settled on its belly. Bernie remembered, "He had tried to release his belly tank, but couldn't, so it blew as soon as he touched. A huge billow of flame went up and the fuel made a path right down to where he stopped. He had skidded several hundred feet before he spilled off to the right side of the runway. The flame just followed him right on down, caught up with him and the A–1E turned into a huge ball of fire. I thought he would get out right away—usually you can get right out and run—but he didn't. It seemed like an awful long while. We estimated about 40 seconds because I made almost a 270-degree turn around him."

Bernie Fisher continued to circle the airstrip and notified the airborne command post that Myers was probably hurt and trapped inside the blazing aircraft. He would learn later that Jump was busy removing his parachute, helmet, gun, and survival kit so he could make a fast exit through the flames. Bernie has vivid memories of the scene on the battletorn runway. "I continued my turn around on the east side of the strip and about that time Jump came out the right side of the airplane. I think the wind must have blown the flames away from the right side. He jumped out and ran, and it looked like he was burning. There was smoke coming from him, but I guess it was because he was so saturated with smoke in that cockpit. He ran toward the end of the wing, jumped off and ran a short distance to the side of the strip."

Jump hid in the brush along one side of the runway opposite the enemy positions on the other side of the strip. He waved as Bernie flew directly overhead. Bernie now knew he was alive, but had no way of knowing if Jump was badly hurt. The airborne command post reported that a rescue helicopter would arrive in 20 minutes.

Bernie and Paco were joined by Captains Jon Lucas and Dennis Hague, and the four Skyraiders made repeated strafing attacks to protect the beleaguered fort and the downed airman.

Ten minutes later, the command post advised that the helicopter was still 20 minutes away and asked Bernie if he could rendezvous with the chopper above the overcast and escort the rescue bird down through the hole in the clouds. Bernie recalls, "I don't think we could have done it. If we had gotten away from there, the VC would have been on him because they were all around him. They controlled the area, but he was pretty well concealed in the brush so they hadn't gotten him."

Bernie made a fateful decision and told the command post he would land and pick Myers up. "They kind of discouraged it. I know it really wasn't wise; it wasn't a very good thing to do, but it is one of those situations you get into. You don't want to do it but you've got to, because he's part of the family; one of our people. You know you have to get him out."

"I told Control I would land, and came right down on the approach. Paco, my wing man, was right along with me, strafing. I was a little too hot—that is a little too fast—and blowing smoke concealed the runway. When I got final I had to fly through the smoke so I kept the power on until I could see what was on the other side. I had a little too much power on. Even though I pulled it off and touched the gear to slow down, I was too far down the runway to stop."

Describing his first landing on the debris-littered runway, Bernie said, "There was all kinds of garbage on there, metal that had blown over from the camp from some of the explosions—tin roofs, buckets and so forth. There were some barrels and somebody had dropped five or six 18-inch diameter rocket pods and I hit a couple of these but I didn't hit anything else. I did a little dodging and weaving and got around the rest, but I was too fast to stop. I knew I would go off the end so I just gave it the power and took it around again."

Bernie made a quick, tight 180° turn and landed in the opposite direction from the first approach. At an altitude of less than 100 feet throughout the maneuver, he wheeled through a hail of enemy fire. "I turned and touched down just about the end of the runway. I used all the brakes I could but the strip was only 2,500 feet long. This is the only time I was scared because it didn't look like I was going to be able to stop. I just hit the brakes as hard as I could and pulled the flaps up which gave me a little more weight on the brakes. I think I must have been skidding on that steel planking. It was a little bit slick from the dampness. I actually went off the end of the runway a little ways. There were a lot of 55-gallon drums sitting out in the weeds and in my mind I was sure I would hit them. My tail did when I turned, but the wing went right over the tops of them."

Fisher taxied at breakneck speed back down the obstacle course and searched for Jump Myers. "I knew about where he was and when I taxied by him he waved both arms vigorously. I stopped as soon as I could but taxiing as fast as I was it must have taken about 100 feet to stop. I waited just a moment expecting him to be right there with me; you know, right on the side. But he wasn't."

"I figured he must be hurt more than I thought—maybe he couldn't move or something—so I set the brakes on the bird and climbed over the right seat to get out on the side he was on. I looked

1 Sep 68
Lt Col William A. Jones III
THE A-1 SKYRAIDERS
Maj Bernard F. Fisher
10 Mar 66
CHINA
BURMA
NORTH VIETNAM
LAOS
THAILAND
CAMBODIA
SOUTH VIETNAM
HAINAN
Ko-chiu
Meng-tzu
P'u-erh
Nan-ning
Mong Cai
Hanoi
Haiphong
Son Tay
Lang Son
Thai Nguyen
Dien Bien Phu
Muang Luong Nam Tha
Houei Sai
Chiang Rai
Samneua
Louangphrabang
Thanh Hoa
Sala Phou Khoun
Muong Sen
Nan
Vinh
Paksane
VIENTIANE
Nong Khai
Udon Thani
Dong Hoi
Tung-fang
Huang-liu
Demarcation Line
Quang Tri
Seno
Savannakhet
Phitsanulok
Khon Kaen
Hue
Da Nang
Nakhon Sawan
Saravane
Ubon Ratchathani
Warin Chamrap
Nakhon Ratchasima
Pakse
Attopeu
Kontum
Pleiku
Prachin Buri
BANGKOK
Chachoengsao
Samut Songkhram
An Nhon
Sisophon
Siem Reap
Stung Treng
Battambang
Kratie
Pursat
Ban Me Thuot
Kompong Cham
Da Lat
PHNOM PENH
Kompong Speu
Svay Rieng
Bien Hoa
SAIGON
Phan Thiet
Sihanoukville
Kampot
My Tho
Vung Tau
Long Xuyen
Vinh Long
Can Tho
Bac Lieu
Quan Long
DAO PHU QUOC (Vietnam)
CON SON
INDOCHINA
Railroad
Road
0 50 100 150 Miles
0 50 100 150 Kilometers
NAMES AND BOUNDARY REPRESENTATION ARE NOT NECESSARILY AUTHORITATIVE

through the mirror and saw two little red, beady eyes trying to crawl up the back of the wing." Bernie grabbed Jump by the seat of the pants and pulled him headfirst onto the floor of the cockpit. "It was hard on his head but he didn't complain," Bernie recalled. Myers said later that he ran as fast as his 46-year-old legs could carry him.

Major Fisher jammed the throttle to the wall and maneuvered the accelerating Skyraider around the shell craters and debris while the North Vietnamese concentrated their fire on the fleeing target. He lifted off at minimum speed and held the bird down on the deck till he had enough speed to pull up into the clouds and head for Pleiku. Bernie learned later that his machine had taken 19 hits from the hostile guns.

The three remaining Skyraiders piloted by Captains Lucas, Hague and Vazquez had made the hair-raising rescue possible by constantly bombing and strafing the enemy. Lucas' bird was hit and badly damaged and all three were out of ammunition as Bernie pulled Jump aboard. They made another low pass at the enemy positions because as Lucas pointed out later, "The VC didn't know we were out of ordnance!" After the battle, 300 Vietcong bodies were counted along the wall of the A Shau outpost.

Another flight of Skyraiders arrived as Bernie Fisher and his three wingmen departed. That afternoon 13 of the 17 Special Forces survivors were successfully evacuated from the fort. Describing the air attacks, one of the survivors said later, "It took all the pressure off the east wall of the fort and enabled us to escape."

September 1, 1968

The road to the command of a flying squadron is long and difficult. Many a lieutenant, fresh out of flying training, begins the journey with high hopes. Twenty years down the road when the opportunity finally comes, only a few are qualified. The chosen few have a history of outstanding performance and a unique blend of flying experience and leadership ability.

To be the boss of a squadron in combat is both a rare honor and a severe challenge. Lieutenant Colonel William A. Jones III got his chance to command in combat 23 years after he began active duty at the end of World War II. His outfit, the 602nd Special Operations Squadron, flew A–1H and A–1J aircraft from Nakhon Phanom Royal Thai Air Force Base.

On the first of September 1968, Bill Jones was required to prove his worth as a man, as a leader, and as a pilot. As dawn broke over Thailand, he took off on his 98th combat mission as Sandy 1, the lead ship in a flight of four A–1s headed west on a search-and-rescue mission. Colonel Jones would be the on-scene commander during the effort to recover a downed F–4 Phantom crew.

Arriving over an area to the northwest of Dong Hoi, North Vietnam, Colonel Jones sent Sandy 3 and 4 into high orbit to remain out of range of the enemy's antiaircraft weapons and to conserve fuel. Colonel Jones and his wingman, Captain Paul A. Meeks, would be the low element, searching for the survivors, locating and destroying the enemy guns, and escorting the helicopters in for the pickup.

As the Sandys crossed Laos inbound to North Vietnam, Liner, a flight of Phantoms, had made radio contact with Carter 02 Alpha, the downed Phantom pilot. Bill Jones recalled, "Liner was able to talk to the survivor. I heard him a little bit on the way in and he thought he knew where the survivor was. Liner flew over, wiggling his wings, but it turned out this was off about eight miles and we got no more contact for almost an hour. We wasted a considerable amount of time—almost an hour—searching in the wrong area."

An F–100 fighter, reestablished radio contact with the downed pilot and directed the Sandys to proceed eight miles to the east. The F–100 pilot warned Colonel Jones that he would be in range of 37-millimeter antiaircraft guns and automatic weapons. Bill knew also that they were close to Route 137, a heavily defended enemy supply road running through North Vietnam into Laos.

The enemy threat was not the only problem Bill Jones and Paul Meeks faced. The survivor's position still had not been pinpointed, and the terrain and weather became more challenging as the A–1s headed east. Below, rugged hills rose abruptly from the valley floor, and above a broken cloud layer obscured the tops of the highest hills.

Nevertheless, there was only one way to find a man hidden in the forbidding countryside. Bill Jones made low pass after low pass crossing the area in a widening search pattern.

Without warning, the A–1 was rocked by a violent explosion from just beneath the fuselage. The North Vietnamese had already found the range. While his cockpit filled with smoke, Bill regained control and jinked from side to side to spoil the gunner's aim. As the smoke cleared, he scanned the instruments and looked the aircraft over. Apparently the Skyraider had been shaken but not seriously damaged by a multi-barreled antiaircraft gun. Once again, the enemy had set up a flak trap for rescue aircraft, using the downed pilot as bait.

Time became a critical factor. The survivor must be located and extracted before the North Vietnamese could beef up their already formidable defenses. Again Bill Jones trolled over the valleys and hillsides as Sandy 2 and the fighters called out the enemy gun positions. His patience and courage were rewarded when Carter 02 Alpha transmitted excitedly that there was an A–1 directly over his position. Bill had found his man.

In the same instant another AA gun opened up on Sandy 1. Again the daring pilot had attracted a barrage of accurate fire. The enemy was actually firing down on the A-1 from the top of a nearby hill.

It was too late for Bill Jones to unleash his own weapons on that pass. He could not risk calling the fighters in for a dive bomb attack on the enemy because the gun position was too close to the downed pilot. Bill racked the Sandy into a tight turn and reversed course, diving back toward his tormentors. He triggered rockets and cannon fire at the hillside, pulled off, and rolled in again.

On the next firing pass, the A–1 was riddled with 14.5 millimeter automatic weapons fire. This time there was no doubt that Colonel Jones was in serious trouble. The rocket motor for the ejection system, located right behind his head, had been ignited by an exploding shell. Bill remembered later, "I looked back over my shoulder and saw fire coming out of the back end of the airplane. The instrument panel was clouded with smoke. Fire seemed to be everywhere. I knew that there wasn't anything for me to do but get out. I pulled for altitude and headed for a clear area. Then I reached down and grabbed the extraction handle with my right hand and pulled. The canopy went off immediately and I waited for the ejection for what seemed like an eternity. But nothing else happened!"

"Here I sat in this thing with fire all around and I said to myself, 'This just can't happen to me. This is not the way it's supposed to be. I've got to get back and see my family. This simply can't happen!' I reached down and grabbed the secondary escape handle, which releases the extraction mechanism, so I could climb out over the side."

The fire burned more intensely when the blast of fresh air hit the cockpit after the canopy was jettisoned. The strap that fastened Bill's oxygen mask burned through, exposing his face to the searing flames. His hands were scorched and Colonel Jones remembered, "They looked like mozzarella cheese!" The cockpit was a smoldering shambles and most of the instruments were unreadable.

Despite the pain, Bill tried desperately to broadcast the exact position of the downed pilot and the hostile guns. His radio calls were blocked as every pilot on the scene screamed at Bill to bail out of the flaming bird. His radio transmitter failed almost immediately and the receiver operated on only one frequency.

As the flames began to die down in the blackened cockpit, Bill Jones had two thoughts. He must make it back to Nakhon Phanom to report the exact location of Carter 02 Alpha and he must not complicate the rescue effort by becoming a survivor himself. He would not bail out!

Paul Meeks joined on the colonel's wing as the two Sandys headed west. Home lay 90 miles and 40 agonizing minutes dead ahead. The two pilots communicated through hand signals and Paul took the lead position.

Having suffered severe burns on his hands, arms, shoulders, neck, and face, Bill Jones flew by instinct. Two-thirds of his windscreen had been shattered by the explosion and the wind-blast on his face caused excruciating pain. His eyes were rapidly swelling shut when Bill trimmed the aircraft to align the remaining portion of the left windscreen with the airstream, affording some protection against the windblast. Now the crippled A–1 was trimmed for uncoordinated flight and skidded through the sky as the ships passed slowly over the Laotian countryside.

Approaching Nakhon Phanom, Paul learned that the weather had deteriorated and the A–1s would have to make a ground-controlled approach through a heavy overcast. Despite his mangled hands and blurred vision, Colonel Jones eased the Skyraider into close formation as Paul led him down throught the clouds.

Bill lowered the landing gear by the emergency system and guided the A–1 to a perfect touchdown and no-flap landing.

Colonel Leonard Volet, the first person to reach the gutted aircraft remembers, "I couldn't believe what I saw. Everything was burned to a crisp, including Colonel Jones' helmet, oxygen mask, survival vest, neck, and arms. Yet, he kept flailing about the cockpit reaching for his maps as we struggled to lift his nearly 200-pound frame and equipment out of the aircraft. We got him out, but he refused medical attention until he was satisfied that we knew where the survivor and guns were located."

The indomitable Bill Jones continued to debrief an intelligence officer as he lay on the operating table.

Meanwhile, near Dong Hai, the massive rescue effort continued. Later that day Carter 02 Alpha was picked up. Bill's supreme effort had not been in vain.

O–1 Aircraft

OV–10 Aircraft

Chapter II. The Forward Air Controllers

The Job

The forward air controller in Vietnam has been cited many times as the single most effective element in spotting the enemy and winning a battle. FACs are the vital link between Air Force attack aircraft and Army ground forces. In Southeast Asia (SEA) they flew the O–1 Bird Dog, the O–2 Super Skymaster, and the OV–10 Bronco in search of the Vietcong. Once the enemy was located, FACs requested approval from proper authorities for tactical air strikes on the target.

The FAC flies low and slow over his target, marks it with smoke grenades or rockets, and calls in strike aircraft or artillery support. He remains near the target, working with the tactical pilots so bombs and other weapons are delivered with maximum precision. Often the opposing forces are separated by only a few meters in the jungle undergrowth, and the utmost accuracy is required to insure the safety of friendly soldiers. Throughout the air strike the FAC remains in radio contact with the Army troops and the strike pilots.

After the attack, the FAC flies in to check battle damage and determine if the target has been successfully destroyed or if more firepower is needed.

A FAC continually flies over the sector of operations of an Army unit. He soon becomes intimately familiar with the terrain, villages, roads, and streams, and his trained eye can detect unusual or suspicious movements. Most FACs have also flown fighters. Familiarity with fighter tactics pays off when they request close air support and control fighter airstrikes.

The FAC was respected and feared by the Vietcong. The enemy knew that whenever he circled overhead, the jungle could erupt from the devastating firepower at his command.

The elusive enemy, the absence of fixed battle lines, and the difficult terrain and weather in Vietnam made effective air and ground coordination mandatory. The FAC provided both protection and offensive firepower for friendly ground troops, who were usually outnumbered when the enemy chose to make contact. At airfields in Vietnam, fighter and attack pilots were on round-the-clock alert, to be scrambled whenever the Army required immediate close air support.

Because of the unique nature of the Vietnam War and the evolution of flexible and responsive air support, it was the first conflict in Air Force history in which a FAC earned the Medal of Honor. The two FACs who won the Medal in Vietnam were killed in action, a fact which underscored the danger inherent in the job.

The Aircraft

Because its mission was to search out the enemy, the O–1E observation aircraft was named the Bird Dog. Built by Cessna, it resembled a Piper Cub in both appearance and performance. The Bird Dog was basically a civilian light plane carrying extra communications gear and four smoke rockets.

The plane measured only 25 feet from propeller to tail wheel. A 213-horsepower engine powered the ship to a top speed of 105 miles per hour. Though capable of reaching altitudes above 18,000 feet, the O–1E usually was flown at low level over the Vietnamese countryside.

The light craft was often buffeted by gusty winds and turbulence, and the cockpit was noisy, cramped, and uncomfortable. Without the benefit of air conditioning, and surrounded by his survival kit, M–16 rifle, sidearm, knife, and maps, the FAC sweltered in the tropical heat and humidity.

The Bird Dog had no offensive firepower, and its thin metal skin offered little protection for the FAC. His skill in maneuvering the tiny craft was the only defense against enemy ground fire. The unsophisticated machine was anything but glamorous, and the FAC would never love the Bird Dog as he did the sleek Super Sabre or the swift Phantom. Though he often looked forward to a return to jet fighter duty, the FAC knew that his job was vital and challenging.

****

The OV–10 is a modern forward air control aircraft with significant improvements over the O–1E. The Bronco's twin turboprop engines give her a top speed of 280 miles per hour, and she carries enough fuel to remain airborne for over four hours. The FAC and backseat observer are protected by a bullet-resistant windscreen, armor plating, and self-sealing fuel tanks. The well-designed cockpit affords both crewmembers unobstructed visibility during air-to-ground operations.

In addition to smoke rockets, the Bronco can carry four 7.62 millimeter mini-guns and over 2,000 pounds of ordnance on external stations. The OV–10 has the maneuverability and endurance for the

FAC mission and the firepower to provide close air support when required.

The Men

In 1950, Hilliard Wilbanks graduated from high school in Cornelia, Georgia. He immediately enlisted in the Air Force and served as a security guard during the Korean War. He began flying in 1954 as an aviation cadet at Laredo, Texas, winning the gold bars of a second lieutenant and the silver wings of an Air Force pilot. Lieutenant Wilbanks flew first as an instructor pilot and then as a fighter pilot in the F–86 Sabre Jet that had become famous in air combat over Korea. He also served in Alaska and Las Vegas, Nevada, as an aircraft maintenance officer.

The fighter pilot became a FAC following training at Hurlburt Field, near Fort Walton Beach, Florida. After assignment to Vietnam in April 1966, the 33-year-old earned the Distinguished Flying Cross and the Air Medal with 18 oak leaf clusters. He was awarded the Medal of Honor posthumously.

****

Steven L. Bennett was born in Palestine, Texas, in April 1946. He entered the Air Force in 1968 and won his wings at Webb Air Force Base, Texas. In 1970, Captain Bennett completed the B–52 bomber training course at Castle Air Force Base, California.

Capt. Hilliard A. Wilbanks

Capt. Steven L. Bennett

He graduated from the FAC and fighter training course at Cannon Air Force Base, New Mexico, before reporting to Vietnam in 1972. The 26-year-old pilot had been in combat less than three months before the Medal of Honor mission. The Medal was awarded posthumously. Captain Bennett also won the Air Medal with three oak leaf clusters.

February 24, 1967

Captain Hilliard A. Wilbanks often flew over the central highlands near Bao Lac and Di Linh. These small cities, located 100 miles northeast of Saigon, were surrounded by a rolling, forested countryside and an occasional plantation. The tribal Montagnards or "mountain people" were the chief inhabitants of the region.

On 24 February 1967, the countryside around Di Linh was not tranquil. The 23rd South Vietnamese Ranger Battalion sought the enemy. They were not alone in the search. A small detachment of American advisers accompanied them, and Americans also patrolled the skies. US Army helicopter gunships hovered nearby while overhead a US Air Force FAC, Hilliard Wilbanks, scanned the terrain that lay before the advancing Rangers.

The Vietcong were ready. The night before they had prepared the perfect ambush site. Local tea plantation workers had been "persuaded" to help them dig foxholes and bunkers on the hills west of Di Linh. From these camouflaged positions they would wreak havoc on February 24.

Early in the day, the VC had decimated one platoon of South Vietnamese troops and hit two other companies hard from the hillside trap. American advisers had been killed, and vital communications gear had been destroyed. Radio contact, that could have warned the advancing 23rd Vietnamese Rangers of the deadly ambush, was no longer possible. As dusk approached, the trap was set again.

By 24 February, Hilliard Wilbanks had completed ten months of the one-year tour in South Vietnam. Two months remained before he could be reunited with his wife and children in the States. But once Hilliard eased the Bird Dog into the air and swung away from the dirt airstrip, there was no time for thoughts of home and family.

As evening approached, he was aloft on his 488th combat mission, contacting Army Captain R. J. Wooten, the senior American adviser with the 23rd Vietnamese Rangers. Captain Wilbanks was also in radio contact with two helicopter gunships hovering west of Di Linh.

As the Rangers advanced slowly through the plantation, the low tea bushes offered them no protective cover. Above, Captain Wilbanks searched the familiar terrain with efficient, probing eyes trained in combat. Suddenly, he saw the trap. The enemy was hidden in camouflaged foxholes on the hillsides; the Rangers were moving toward the ambush. Captain Wooten's radio crackled with the FAC's warning just as the hillsides erupted with enemy fire. The trap was sprung again.

Later, Captain Wooten said, "My lead elements, working their way up the slope, were unaware of the VC positions just ahead until Captain Wilbanks told us. Realizing their ambush was discovered, the VC opened up on my forces and the two FAC planes above with mortars, machine guns, automatic rifles, and countless shoulder weapons. Two of my companies were pinned down and the forward elements suffered heavy casualties."

Overhead the Bird Dog banked and turned as Hilliard fired a white phosphorous rocket toward the center of the enemy fire. The marking smoke rose from the hillside, pinpointing the ambush site, and the two helicopter gunships wheeled toward the enemy, fired rapidly, and pulled away. A third chopper was hit by .50-caliber fire, which damaged its hydraulic system. Wilbanks advised the remaining pair of gunships to escort the crippled craft to friendly territory. A second FAC radioed that two flights of fighters were on the way. Their firepower was desperately needed.

Then Captain Wilbanks saw movement. The Vietcong had abandoned their foxholes. With bayonets and knives ready, they charged down the slope toward the badly outnumbered Rangers. There was scant hope for help from the air since the gunships had departed and the fighters would not arrive in time. The Vietnamese and American soldiers would never forget the next few minutes.

The FAC was overhead once more. A smoke rocket exploded amidst the enemy force. The Vietcong turned their attention skyward and sent a hail of bullets toward the fleeing Bird Dog. Again Wilbanks banked his plane toward the enemy. He had their full attention now as another smoke rocket slammed into the hillside. The Bird Dog had become the hunter! Yet another low pass followed, and again intense groundfire threatened the aircraft. Wilbanks fired another rocket, his last. He knew it. The Rangers knew it. The enemy knew it. The FAC had done it all, risking his life to inflict casualties on the enemy and to protect the Rangers. It was time for him to pull off the target and wait for the fighters. But Hilliard Wilbanks was not finished.

He had one threat left in the automatic rifle that he carried as a survival weapon. Now Captain Wilbanks became both a pilot and a rifleman. Pointing the O–1 toward the enemy, he released the controls and fired his rifle from the side window. As the Bird Dog careened above the tree tops, he grabbed the controls to recover the plane and evade the enemy's fire. Now the Vietcong were off-balance and confused. The FAC reloaded another clip and attacked again. "Each pass he was so close we could hear his plane being hit," said Captain Wooten. The second FAC tried to contact Captain Wilbanks, but there was no reply. On the third rifle-firing pass the aerial ballet ended.

A Ranger adviser, Captain Gary F. Vote, said, "He was no more than 100 feet off the ground and almost over his objective, firing his rifle. Then he began the erratic moves, first up, then down, then banking west right over my position. I thought he was wounded and looking for a friendly spot to land. I jumped up and waved my arms. But as he banked again, I could see that he was unconscious. His aircraft crashed about 100 meters away." The fallen Bird Dog came to rest in no man's land between the two forces.

Captain Wilbanks was alive when Captain Vote pulled him from the wreckage. Meanwhile, the two helicopter gunships that doubled as rescue birds returned. They fired their remaining ammunition into the enemy positions and swooped low toward the fallen Bird Dog to pick up the FAC. Four times they tried to set down in no man's land. Four times the Vietcong guns drove them off.

Under the direction of another FAC, two Phantom fighters raked the enemy with 20-millimeter cannon fire. At last a helicopter, braving the withering groundfire, picked up Hilliard Wilbanks. He died in the chopper en route to the treatment center at Bao Lac.

June 29, 1972

On 29 June, Captain Steve Bennett and his backseat observer, Captain Mike Brown, prepared for a combat mission. Mike was a Marine Corps company commander stationed in Hawaii. He had volunteered for temporary duty in Vietnam to assist Air Force FACs in directing naval gunfire. At about 3 p.m., the Air Force-Marine team took off from Danang Air Base and headed northwest along the coast. Thirty minutes later they arrived at Quang Tri and began to circle beneath a deck of low clouds.

For the next two hours, the OV–10 crew adjusted naval artillery from US ships in the Gulf of Tonkin. Mike's radioed instructions to the heavy cruiser *Newport News* and the destroyer *R.B. Anderson*, allowed the ships to pinpoint their fire against positions near Quang Tri.

It was time for Steve to turn the Bronco to the south and head for home when he learned that his relief had been delayed on the ground at Danang. A quick check of the fuel gauges confirmed what Steve already knew. He had enough gas to remain on station for another hour. Steve and Mike went back to work.

While darkness approached, Steve controlled two flights of Navy A–6 Intruder jet fighters in support of South Vietnamese ground troops. As he worked the second flight, the cloud deck caused a problem. With their maneuvering space severely limited by the low ceiling, the A–6 pilots had difficulty lining up with the target. Steve fired a second smoke rocket to make certain that the fighters would deliver their ordnance where he wanted it. When the Intruders completed their last attack and headed seaward toward their carrier, Steve and Mike surveyed the results of the strike.

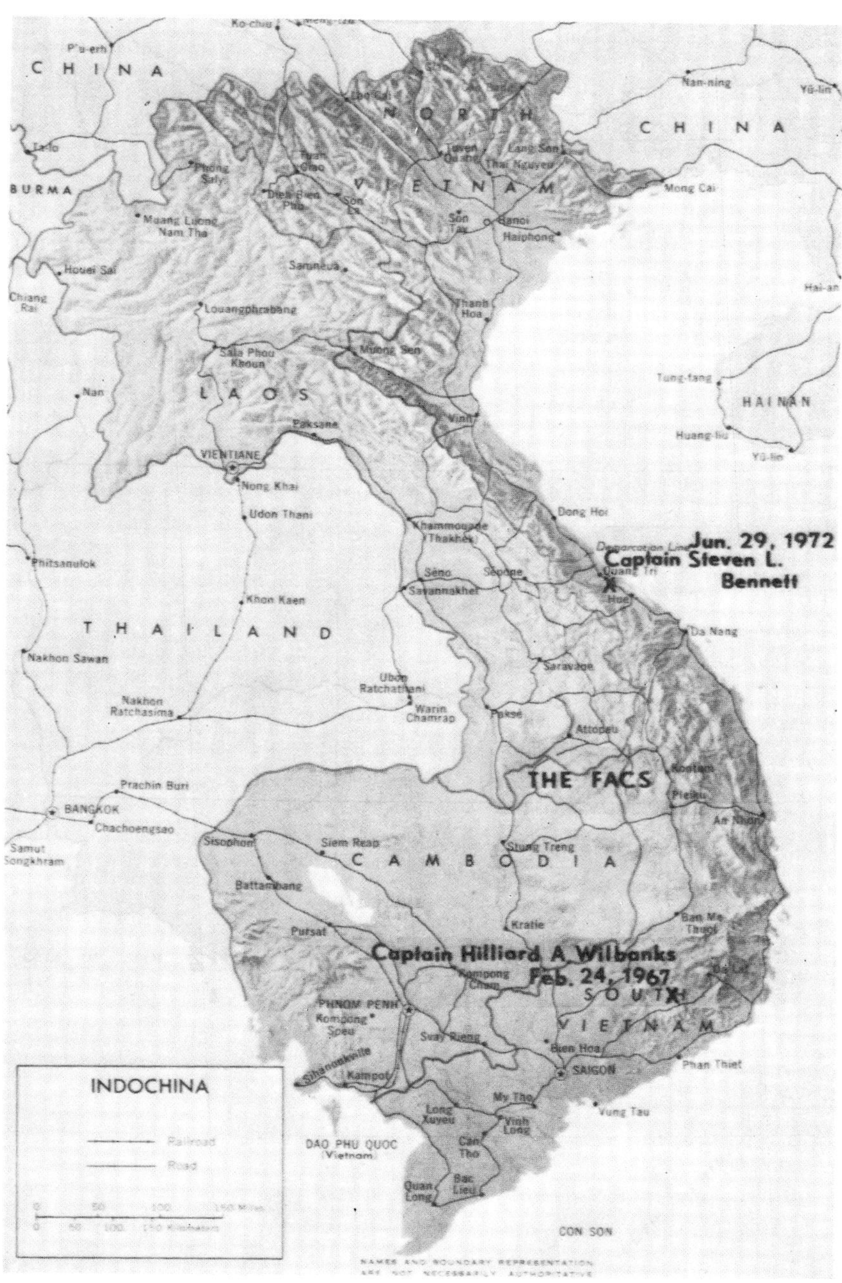

CHINA
NORTH
VIETNAM
CHINA
BURMA
Nan-ning
Mong Cai
Hanoi
Haiphong
Son Tay
Muang Luong Nam Tha
Houei Sai
Chiang Rai
Louangphrabang
Thanh Hoa
Muong Sen
LAOS
Nan
Vinh
Tung-fang
HAINAN
Huang-liu
VIENTIANE
Nong Khai
Udon Thani
Dong Hoi
Jun. 29, 1972
Captain Steven L. Bennett
Quang Tri
Hue
Da Nang
Phitsanulok
Khon Kaen
THAILAND
Nakhon Sawan
Ubon Ratchathani
Warin Chamrap
Nakhon Ratchasima
Saravane
Pakse
Attopeu
THE FACS
Kontum
Pleiku
An Nhon
Prachin Buri
BANGKOK
Chachoengsao
Samut Songkhram
Sisophon
Siem Reap
Stung Treng
CAMBODIA
Battambang
Kratie
Ban Me Thuot
Pursat
Captain Hilliard A. Wilbanks
Feb. 24, 1967
Kompong Cham
Da Lat
SOUTH
VIETNAM
PHNOM PENH
Kompong Speu
Svay Rieng
Bien Hoa
SAIGON
Phan Thiet
Kampot
My Tho
Vung Tau
Vinh Long
Long Xuyen
Can Tho
DAO PHU QUOC (Vietnam)
Bac Lieu
Quan Long
CON SON
INDOCHINA
Railroad
Road
NAMES AND BOUNDARY REPRESENTATION ARE NOT NECESSARILY AUTHORITATIVE

A mile to the south, a South Vietnamese platoon of about two dozen men was pinned down at a fork in a creek. Several hundred North Vietnamese Army regulars advanced along the creek bank toward their position. The enemy was supported by a heavy artillery barrage and protected by antiaircraft artillery and heat-seeking surface-to-air (SA 7) missiles. The platoon's situation was desperate when a US Marine ground artillery spotter radioed an emergency call for assistance.

Steve Bennett heard the call and responded immediately, swinging the OV–10 toward the fork in the creek. There were no fighters in the area to help. Naval gunfire would threaten the friendly troops as well as the North Vietnamese. Steve had only his skill, the Bronco's four machine guns, and 2,000 rounds of ammunition to pit against the enemy. He would have to attack at low altitude, where the hostile antiaircraft weapons were most effective. Steve radioed for permission to use his guns and got it.

Each time the FAC dove toward the creek bank, he met heavy return fire. After his fourth strafing pass, the North Vietnamese began to pull back, leaving many of their dead and wounded behind. The Bronco had taken several small arms hits in the fuselage, but Steve decided to press the attack to prevent the enemy from regrouping. As he pulled off after the fifth pass, their luck ran out.

Neither Steve nor Mike had any warning as the SA 7 struck from behind. The OV–10 shuddered as the missile hit the left engine and exploded. Steve struggled to control the aircraft as the cockpit was bombarded with shrapnel and debris. Though the canopy was full of holes, he had not been hit. Mike had minor wounds on his hand, head, and back. Together they surveyed the crippled craft. Much of the left engine was gone, and the left landing gear, which had been retracted in a compartment behind the engine, was now hanging limply in the airstream. Worst of all, they were afire!

Steve knew he must jettison the remaining smoke rockets and the external fuel tank before the fire caused an explosion which could destroy the aircraft. He should jettison the stores immediately, but to do so would endanger the lives of the South Vietnamese Marines who were spread out between his present position and the coast. He began a race against time, heading for open water.

In the meantime, Mike had transmitted a distress message on the emergency radio channel. "May Day! May Day! This is Wolfman four-five with Covey eight-seven. We are in the vicinity of Triple Nickel (Highway 555) and 602, heading out feet wet."

The Bronco was a handful for Steve. He consistently fought the controls to maintain straight and level flight as the remaining engine strained to bank and turn the aircraft. Unable to gain altitude, they passed just 600 feet above the beach and the American ships. Reaching open water at last, Steve jettisoned the fuel tank and rockets as he and Mike prepared to eject.

Looking over his shoulder, Mike discovered that his parachute was gone. "What I saw was a hole about a foot square from the rocket blast, and bits of my parachute shredded up and down the cargo bay," Mike says. "I told Steve I couldn't jump." Suddenly there was hope, as the flames subsided.

Quickly the FAC turned southeast down the coast. The landing strips at Phu Bai and Hue were closest, but the battered Bronco would need the foamed runway and crash equipment at Danang. As they passed the city of Hue, the fire flared again and a pilot in a chase plane confirmed that the OV–10 was dangerously close to exploding.

Realizing that they would never reach Danang and that Mike could not eject without a chute, Steve decided to ditch the Bronco by crash-landing in the water. He knew that an OV–10 pilot had never survived a ditching and that the aircraft was likely to break up in the cockpit area as it struck the water. A squadron pilot would later recall, "We talked about it a lot in pilot shop talk. Punch out or get it on dry land, or whatever you can do, but don't ditch it."

Steve eased the aircraft into a slow descent toward the water as the two captains completed their pre-ditching checklist. They touched down about one mile from a sandy beach and Mike remembers, "We dug in harder than hell." The landing gear caught in the sea before the Bronco cartwheeled and flipped over on its back.

In the submerged rear cockpit, Mike labored frantically to free himself. He unstrapped and tried to exit through the top of the canopy. Finding the way blocked, he pulled himself clear through an opening in the side and yanked the toggles to inflate his life preserver. On the surface, Mike found only the aircraft's tail section still afloat.

He swam around the tail but could not find Steve. Mike pulled himself down the tail section and back underwater, fighting to reach the front cockpit. He got only as far as the wing, and when he surfaced for the second time, the OV–10 had gone under. A few minutes later, at about 7 p.m., Mike Brown was picked up by a Navy rescue helicopter.

The next day, 30 June, Steve Bennett's body was recovered from the smashed cockpit of the submerged aircraft. He had had no chance to escape.

Chapter III. The Wild Weasels

The Job

Former Air Force Chief of Staff General J.P. McConnell described the area around Hanoi, North Vietnam as having "the greatest concentration of aircraft weapons that has ever been known in the history of defense of any area in the world." The job of the wild weasels was to combat these awesome defenses to protect American aircraft striking key targets in the north.

The weasel aircraft and crew were well suited for their hazardous mission. The two-seat fighter bombers carried sophisticated electronic gear and weapons to help the pilot and his backseat electronic warfare officer or "bear" locate and destroy enemy surface-to-air missile (SAM) and antiaircraft artillery (AAA) sites. The weasel crew was alerted to a hostile radar signal by a rattlesnake-like tone in the headset and a bright blip on the warning scope. They could attack by unleashing a radar-homing air-to-ground missile from a comparatively safe distance or by diving directly over the site to drop conventional bombs.

The experienced North Vietnamese missile crews could decoy the defense suppression birds by sending all the electronic indications of a SAM launch without actually firing the missile. Thus, when the warning scope was cluttered with many threat indications, the weasels could never be sure where and when the next SAM would be fired. The pilot and bear had constantly to scan the horizon in all directions to find the deadly "telephone poles" rising to meet them so the pilot could pull the aircraft into the violent maneuvers required to evade the SAM. Their big fear was the SAM fired from a site directly behind the aircraft that might streak in unnoticed to send a lethal blast through the weasel bird.

The flak-and-SAM-suppression job was inherently dangerous. The weasels deliberately flew in range of the North Vietnamese defenses to force the enemy gunners and missile crews to commit themselves. While concentrating on the surface threat, they could never forget that MIG interceptors lurked nearby waiting for the chance to sneak in undetected and rip the American aircraft with air-to-air missiles or cannon fire.

The wild weasel crews had earned the respect of their comrades. In the north, every vital target was protected by bristling defenses, but the weasels constantly took death-defying risks to attack these defenses and thereby protect the main strike force.

The Aircraft

The Republic-built F–105 Thunderchief was designed to be a nuclear strike fighter bomber with a limited capability for air-to-air combat. The F–105's internal bomb bay was as large as that of the World War II B–17. This single-engine bird was big for a fighter, weighing over 25 tons with a full load. Called the "lead sled" by some pilots because of her size and weight, the Thunderchief was aerodynamically clean, and could break the sound barrier at low level and streak at more than twice the speed of sound at high altitude. Modern electronic and navigation equipment gave the bird an all-weather mission capability, while unique "tape-measure" gauges replaced the standard round-dial instruments.

F–105 Aircraft

The rugged fighter got its first combat test in Vietnam, where pilots affectionately nicknamed her the "Thud." With six tons of ordnance and 1,000 rounds of ammunition for the 20-millimeter cannon, the Thud proved to be a formidable and reliable machine, carrying many pilots safely through 100 missions over the heavily defended north. Launching from bases in Thailand and refueling in the air over Laos, the Thuds would strike deep in the Red River Valley heartland of North Vietnam. With superior speed at low altitude, they could outrace the MIG interceptors and maneuver to evade the SAM missiles.

The mountain range northwest of Hanoi became famous as "Thud Ridge," providing an easily recognizable checkpoint for navigation and a natural shield which protected the F–105s from the bristling defenses. Several 105s, having been hit by flak or SAMs over Hanoi, crashed to flaming destruction on the slopes of Thud Ridge.

Though the F–105 fighter wings in Thailand were composed primarily of single-seat aircraft, the two-seat Thuds, manned by the pilot-and-electronic-warfare-officer team, were ideal for the wild weasel role.

The Men

Merlyn Hans Dethlefsen was born in Greenville, Iowa, on June 29, 1934. After attending the University of Omaha, he entered the Air Force and began aviation cadet training in 1954.

Captain Dethlefsen served a tour of duty as a fighter pilot in Germany before transferring to a combat squadron in Thailand in October 1966. The 33-year-old officer won the Medal on his 78th combat mission, exactly one year after Major Fisher earned the first Air Force Medal of Honor of the Vietnam War.

Before finishing his tour in Southeast Asia, Captain Dethlefsen also earned the Distinguished Flying Cross and the Air Medal with nine oak leaf clusters.

****

Leo K. Thorsness was born in Walnut Grove, Minnesota, on February 14, 1932. He enlisted in the Air Force in 1951 and won his wings and a commission in 1954. Completing his education in the service, he graduated from the University of Omaha in 1964 and earned a master's degree from the University of Southern California in 1966.

The veteran airman was an F–105 instructor pilot at Las Vegas, Nevada, before he was assigned to Thailand in October 1966. Eleven days after the Medal of Honor mission, Major Thorsness was shot down over North Vietnam on his 93rd mission, just seven short of the 100 required for a complete combat tour.

After almost six years of captivity, Lieutenant Colonel Leo Thorsness and his backseater, Major Harry Johnson, were released in March 1973. Six months later, Leo was presented the Medal of Honor, and

Capt. Merlyn H. Dethlefsen

Maj. Leo K. Thorsness

he retired shortly thereafter. During his extraordinary career he was awarded the Silver Star, the Distinguished Flying Cross with five oak leaf clusters, the Air Medal with nine clusters, and the Purple Heart with one cluster. He shot down one MIG fighter during the Vietnam War.

March 10, 1967

On March 10, 1967, a flight of F–105 Thunderchiefs took off from Takhli Royal Thai Air Force Base. Captain Merlyn Hans Dethlefsen eased the number three Thud into position as the four-ship formation headed north. This was his 78th combat mission.

Over 500 miles away, in the North Vietnamese heartland, lay the Thai Nguyen steel mill and industrial complex. Nestled in a valley 40 miles north of Hanoi, and 70 miles from the Red Chinese border, the heavily defended complex was a vital cog in Ho Chi Minh's war machine. It had only recently been approved as a target for US fighter-bombers.

Four Thunderchiefs, with the call sign "Lincoln," were scheduled to be the first flight on target that day. Their mission was to knock out the lethal defenses that ringed the target: surface to air missiles (SAMs), antiaircraft artillery (AAA), and automatic weapons. There was also a good possibility that the Thuds would be greeted by Soviet- and Chinese-built MIG interceptors.

The flight leader and Captain Dethlefsen each piloted two-seat Thunderchiefs for the wild weasel mission. As they neared hostile territory the back seater, or "bear," would be busy scanning his gear for the telltale signals that could pinpoint North Vietnamese defenses.

On schedule, the F–105 pilots rendezvoused with a tanker and refueled. They departed the tanker just five minutes ahead of the main strike force and prepared to cross the enemy border, hoping the good weather would hold.

Fighter pilots who had survived many missions over the north had developed a sound combat tactic. They would strike the target quickly, delivering their ordnance on one pass, then pull off, using maximum power and violent evasive maneuvers, to head for home. Merl Dethlefsen had used this formula many times and had never been hit by flak. Those who attempted a second pass on the target often did not live to tell about it.

Lincoln had guided his formation at medium altitude to the north of Thai Nguyen. About two miles from the target, they zoomed for altitude and rolled into a steep diving attack on the active SAM site. Merl and his wingman were nearly a mile behind the first element when they lost sight of the leader in the most intense flak imaginable. The number two ship broke hard to the right and Merl followed. A moment later, the parachute beeper signal on the emergency radio channel confirmed that the lead crew had ejected from their crippled aircraft.

Number two, trying desperately to escape from the hornet's nest around Thai Nguyen, reported that his Thud had been badly damaged.

Merl Dethlefsen took command of the flight. He remembers, "We were still ahead of the strike force and they (the strike force) were still vulnerable. We had fuel and missiles, guns and bombs, and the job wasn't done yet. Lincoln lead had seen the target and launched a missile, but it had missed. I decided we would stay. Coming around, I studied the flak pattern. It wasn't a matter of being able to avoid the flak, but of finding the least-intense areas."

Captain Dethlefsen's wingman, Major Kenneth Bell recalls, "We sometimes had targets where we got no flak at all. Apparently the enemy didn't care about them. But this one was different. When we got that kind of greeting at Thai Nguyen you know we were hitting something they wanted to hang on to. It was a vital target and its loss would hurt them."

Merl and his backseater, Captain Kevin "Mike" Gilroy, had located the approximate position of the SAM site on the first pass. As he maneuvered the aircraft to line up with the target, Merl spotted two MIG-21s closing fast from the rear quadrant. He fired his radar-seeking missile at the SAM site and veered sharply away as one of the MIGs triggered a missile toward the Thud.

Dethlefsen described how he shook off the attackers, "I broke to the right, down through the flak. I figured that would give me the best chance of evading both the heat-seeking missile and the MIGs' guns. Didn't think the MIGs would want to follow me through that stuff. They didn't."

It was standard procedure for F–105 pilots under attack by MIGs to jettison their ordnance, engage the afterburner, and head for the treetops, where the Thud could outrace the interceptors. The heavy fighter bomber was no match for the maneuverable MIG in a dogfight.

As Merl repositioned for another pass he saw two more MIG–21s and evaded them with a tight left break. He elected to retain his ordnance, but now he had another problem.

The antiaircraft artillery had taken its toll. At least one of the 57-millimeter gunners had scored a bullseye, jolting the Thud with a direct hit. Miraculously, the flight controls and engine responded normally as Captain Dethlefsen checked his aircraft out. Chunks of shrapnel through the bottom of the Thud's fuselage and the left wingtip had not damaged any of her vital systems. The two-man crew again turned their attention to the SAM site, and Merl remembers that the main force was already leaving the industrial complex.

"I could hear the strike force withdrawing. I had permission to stay there after they left. That steel mill with the related industry was a big target—too big to knock out with one strike. I knew those fighter-bombers would be back tomorrow. Same route, right over this area. My aircraft was working well enough to be effective. With the weather the way it was that day I knew we would never have a better chance. So I made up my mind to stay until I got that SAM site or they got me."

Maneuvering around the flak pattern, Merl spotted another SAM site dead ahead. He squeezed off a missile and the SAM radar shut down.

Smoke and dust from the main strike on the complex began to drift over the defensive positions as the pilot and his bear strained to spot the original SAM site. Merl eased the streaking Thunderchief down on the deck for a better look.

Throughout the harrowing sequence of events, Ken Bell had stuck to his leader like glue. His 105 had been hit by both AAA and a MIG. Because of a damaged aileron, Ken could turn his Thud only to the right as he followed Merlyn Dethlefsen down the chute once more.

At last the weasel delivered the knockout punch. Merl dropped his bombs squarely on the site and followed with a cannon pass, his 20-millimeter gun blazing away. The SAM site burned as the 105s pulled off.

The two battle-weary Thuds sped toward the tanker and home station. Pilots who would fly over Thai Nguyen on another day were glad that Captain Dethlefsen had stayed.

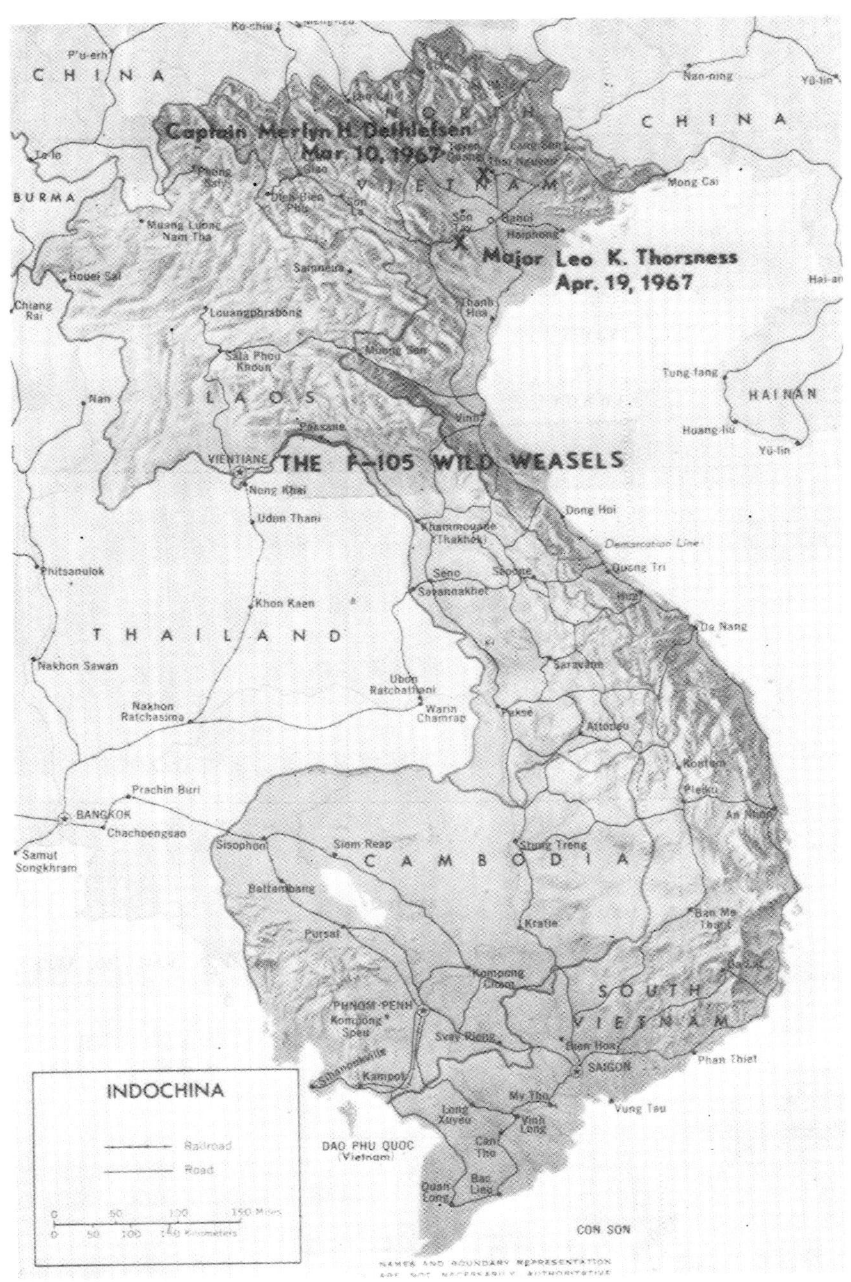

Ko-chiu
P'u-erh
C H I N A
Nan-ning
Yü-lin
C H I N A
Captain Merlyn H. Dethlefsen
Mar. 10, 1967
N O R T H
V I E T N A M
Tuyen Quang
Lang Son
Thai Nguyen
Mong Cai
BURMA
Phong Saly
Dien Bien Phu
Son La
Son Tay
Hanoi
Haiphong
Muang Luong Nam Tha
Major Leo K. Thorsness
Apr. 19, 1967
Houei Sai
Samneua
Hai-an
Chiang Rai
Louangphrabang
Thanh Hoa
Sala Phou Khoun
Muong Sen
Tung-fang
Nan
L A O S
HAINAN
Vinh
Paksane
Huang-liu
Yü-lin
VIENTIANE
THE F-105 WILD WEASELS
Nong Khai
Udon Thani
Dong Hoi
Khammouane (Thakhek)
Demarcation Line
Phitsanulok
Seno
Quang Tri
Savannakhet
Hue
Khon Kaen
Da Nang
T H A I L A N D
Nakhon Sawan
Saravane
Ubon Ratchathani
Nakhon Ratchasima
Warin Chamrap
Pakse
Attopeu
Kontum
Prachin Buri
Pleiku
BANGKOK
An Nhon
Chachoengsao
Samut Songkhram
Sisophon
Siem Reap
Stung Treng
C A M B O D I A
Battambang
Ban Me Thuot
Kratie
Pursat
Da Lat
Kompong Cham
S O U T H
PHNOM PENH
Kompong Speu
V I E T N A M
Svay Rieng
Bien Hoa
Sihanoukville
Phan Thiet
SAIGON
Kampot
INDOCHINA
My Tho
Vung Tau
Long Xuyen
Vinh Long
Railroad
Can Tho
Road
DAO PHU QUOC (Vietnam)
Bac Lieu
Quan Long
0 50 100 150 Miles
0 50 100 150 Kilometers
CON SON
NAMES AND BOUNDARY REPRESENTATION ARE NOT NECESSARILY AUTHORITATIVE

"All I did was the job I was sent to do," Dethlefsen said. "It had been quite a while since we had been able to go into the Hanoi area. So while the weather held we were able to do some pretty good work. It was a case of doing my job to the best of my ability. I think that is what we mean when we call ourselves professional airmen in the Air Force."

Merl Dethlefsen's understatement of his heroic contribution reflects the attitude of the pilots who risked their lives daily over the north. Each considered himself a part of the team. The destruction of vital targets in the enemy's stronghold would never be a one-man operation.

April 19, 1967

Six weeks after Captain Dethlefsen had silenced the enemy defenses around Thai Nguyen, another weasel pilot took off from Takhli. Major Leo K. Thorsness and his back-seater, Captain Harold E. Johnson, were nearing the 100-mission mark that would bring their combat tour to an end.

Leo was the "old head" weasel pilot at Takhli and the instructor for newly assigned crews. MIGs had chased Leo and Harry through the skies of North Vietnam, and the experienced pair had evaded 53 SAMs. Describing the flak-and-SAM-suppression missions, Leo said, "In essence, we would go in high enough to let somebody shoot at us and low enough to go down and get them; then we went in and got them." The weasels would be the first flight on target, preceding the main attack and remaining after the strike force had departed. It was like trolling for sharks in a canoe!

On 19 April 1967, Leo led his flight of four Thuds from the tanker in southern Laos toward the North Vietnamese border. They were headed for the Xuan Mai army barracks and storage supply area 30 miles to the southwest of Hanoi. Xuan Mai lay on the edge of the Red River delta, where rice paddies give way to forested mountains. Hopefully, the defenses would not be as lethal as those ringing downtown Hanoi.

The rattlesnake tone in Leo's headset buzzed in time with the flickering strobes on Harry's scope. The eerie sound signalled that already the enemy missile crews were warming up the SAM radars and searching for American aircraft. The rattlesnake whined louder and the strobes got bigger as the weasels flew deeper into North Vietnam.

Though the bear's warning gear detected the SAM tracking and guidance radars, the weasel crews had no guaranteed cockpit indication of a launch. If they were lucky, they would spot the lethal "telephone pole" rising from its pad in a cloud of dust. If they were not so lucky, they would find the missile while there was still time to avoid it with a desperation maneuver. If their luck had run out, the missile would streak in undetected from behind, and its high-explosive warhead would shatter the unsuspecting Thunderchief.

Leo sent his number 3 and 4 men to the north of Xuan Mai as he and number 2 headed to the south. Now the enemy gunners would be forced to divide their attention between the separated flights.

Major Thorsness maneuvered toward a strong SAM signal and fired a radar-seeking Shrike missile. The site was seven miles distant and obscured by haze, so Leo and Harry never saw the missile hit. But the abrupt disappearance of the enemy's signal from Harry's scope indicated that the Shrike had probably done its job.

Leo picked up a second SAM site visually and rolled into a diving attack through a curtain of AAA fire. He pickled his CBUs (cluster bomb units) dead on target and pulled out of the steep dive.

The two Thuds accelerated toward the treetops where they would have the best chance for survival. But number 2 was in trouble. Antiaircraft rounds had found Tom Madison's machine, and the glowing overheat light confirmed that his engine had been hit. Leo told Tom to head for the hills to the west, but the rescue beeper on guard (emergency) radio channel signalled that Madison and his back-seater, Tom Sterling, had already bailed out. Somehow Leo found time in the midst of the emergency to fire another Shrike at a third SAM site.

To the north numbers 3 and 4 had survived an air battle with MIG interceptors. Number 3's afterburner would not light, and without the added thrust the flight could not sustain the supersonic speed to outrun their attackers. Somehow 3 and 4 staved off two more MIGs as they limped south toward Takhli. Leo's Thud was now the only fighter-bomber in the Xuan Mai area.

Major Thorsness circled the descending parachutes while Harry relayed information to "Crown," the rescue control aircraft. Suddenly Harry spotted a MIG off their left wing, and Leo recalls, "I wasn't sure whether or not he was going to attack the parachutes. So I said, 'Why not?' and took off after him. I was a little high, dropped down to 1,000 feet and headed north behind him. I was driving right up his tailpipe at 550 knots. At about 3,000 feet I opened up on him with the 20 millimeter but completely missed him. We attacked again, and I was pulling and holding the trigger when Harry got my attention with the MIGs behind us. If I had hit that MIG good, we would have swallowed some of the explosion (debris). But we got him."

Low on gas, Leo sped south toward the tanker, following the progress of the rescue forces on his radio. The prop-driven Sandys that would direct the on-scene effort and the rescue helicopters that would attempt the pick-up were already headed toward the downed weasel crew.

With full tanks but with only 500 rounds of ammunition, Leo left the tanker and flew north again. While briefing the Sandy pilots on the defenses around Xuan Mai, he spotted three interceptors ahead.

"One of the MIGs flew right into my gunsight at about 2,000 feet and pieces started falling off the (enemy) aircraft. They hadn't seen us, but they did now."

Harry warned that four MIGs were closing from the rear and Leo dove for the deck, eluding his pursuers as the Thud raced through the mountain passes with the afterburner blazing.

Now the MIGs turned back toward the slow-moving Sandys and Thorsness radioed a warning, "Okay, Sandy One. Just keep that machine of yours turning and they can't get you." Low on fuel again and without ammunition, Leo turned toward the MIGs with one idea in mind: "To try to get them on me." He knew the Sandys would be sitting ducks for the MIGs.

At last a flight of 105s arrived, and now the MIGs were on the defensive. By evening, the Americans claimed the MIG that Leo had killed plus four probables, including the enemy aircraft that had flown in front of Leo's deadly guns.

The 1,000-foot flames and billowing smoke from Xuan Mai could be seen over 40 miles away—a silent testimony to the success of the airstrike.

But Major Thorsness was far from satisfied as he flew toward the tanker for the third time. A Sandy had been shot down, and the rescue effort for Madison and Sterling had been called off. Both were later captured. Now Leo faced yet another crucial decision.

"Leo, I'm not with the rest of the flight, and I don't know where I am. I've only got 800 pounds (of fuel). What should I do?" It was a fellow Thud pilot in trouble.

"I've never felt so sorry for anyone," recounts Thorsness. "It wasn't unusual to get lost in battle, and any number of things could happen in a fight to use an awful lot of fuel. But it sounded like I would have to do something magic."

What Leo did was send the tanker north toward the lost pilot. Thankfully, the rendezvous was successful and the pilot plugged into the tanker before the gas-gulping engine flamed out from fuel starvation. But now Leo was critically low on gas as he continued south toward the nearest recovery base at Udorn, Thailand.

"I knew if we could get to the Mekong River—the Fence—we could coast across. With 70 miles to go, I pulled the power back to idle and we just glided in. We were indicating 'empty' when the runway came up just in front of us, and we landed a little long. As we climbed out of the cockpit, Harry said something quaint like, 'That's a full day's work!' "

Chapter IV. The Helicopters

The Job

In Vietnam, the helicopter was a vital cog in the American fighting machine. Choppers were used extensively by the Army as troop carriers, to move the foot soldier into contact with the elusive enemy, and as gunships, to provide firepower for forward combat units. Air Force helicopters were used primarily in the rescue role, often penetrating deep into North Vietnam to snatch downed airmen from the enemy's own backyard.

The daring pickups in hostile territory resulted from the teamwork of a dedicated and responsive rescue force. Within seconds after the scramble order was received, the helicopters and the propeller-driven Sandys were airborne. In the pickup area, the Sandys suppressed the enemy groundfire to protect the downed pilot and the vulnerable choppers. The rescue was coordinated by the crew of an HC-130P airborne command post. The big cargo bird was also a tanker, able to refuel the helicopters during a long rescue mission.

In the ideal situation the rescue birds could locate the downed airman quickly by homing in on the electronic signal from his emergency locater beacon. Contacting the Sandys on his survival radio, the survivor would authenticate his identity to prevent an English-speaking North Vietnamese from using the emergency frequency to lure American aircraft into a flak trap.

After moving in for the pickup, the hovering helicopter would often lower the cable directly to the jungle hiding place, hoisting the pilot to safety through the dense foliage. If he was injured, a paramedic would descend on the pickup device to help him aboard.

Their business was never routine, and the rescue crews risked their lives daily in keeping with their motto, "That others may live." The combat fighter pilot slept better at night knowing that if he was shot down, the rescue force would get him out if it was humanly possible.

The Air Force also used some helicopters for special missions.

HH–3 Aircraft

UH–1 Aircraft

These utility choppers had flown in the states supporting Strategic Air Command's remote missile sites. In Vietnam the armed birds carried Army Special Forces teams to isolated landing zones in Vietcong-controlled areas.

After the green berets had observed enemy activity, they would rendezvous with the helicopter at a predetermined time for pickup and evacuation. If the small team was attacked by a large enemy force, they would radio the transport birds for immediate pickup.

The Aircraft

The versatile Sikorsky HH-3E "Jolly Green Giant" could operate from land or water. The big rescue ship was manned by a crew of four and armed with two mini-machineguns. Weighing over 11 tons, the cargo version could carry a 5,000-pound load or 25 combat-ready troops. Twin turbine engines powered the chopper at a top speed of 165 miles per hour.

Ideally suited for the rescue mission, the Jolly was equipped with armor plating and self-sealing fuel tanks to protect the crew when the hovering bird was hit by groundfire. With inflight refueling, the chopper had unlimited range and endurance.

****

The Bell UH-1 light utility helicopter was used extensively by the Air Force, Army, and Marines in Vietnam. With a one- or two-man crew, the Huey could carry a payload of 4,000 pounds or 10 passengers at a top speed of 115 miles per hour. A modified version, carrying machineguns or rocket launchers, served as an Army gunship.

The Men

Gerald O. Young was born in Chicago on May 19, 1930. He served as a Navy enlisted man before entering Air Force aviation cadet training. Lieutenant Young won his wings and a commission in 1958.

Captain Young reported for rescue helicopter duty in Vietnam in 1967. The 37-year-old pilot won the Medal of Honor on his 60th combat mission.

****

James P. Fleming was born in Sedalia, Missouri, on March 12, 1943. He was commissioned through the Reserve Officers Training Corps program upon graduation from Washington State University in 1966.

Capt. Gerald O. Young

1st Lt. James P. Fleming

First Lieutenant Fleming was assigned to helicopter duty in Vietnam in July 1968. The 25-year-old had been an Air Force pilot less than two years when he won the Medal. Before completing his Southeast Asia tour in May 1969, Lieutenant Fleming flew 810 helicopter sorties in combat.

In addition to the Medal of Honor, he earned the Silver Star, the Distinguished Flying Cross, and the Air Medal with seven oak leaf clusters.

November 9, 1967

It was around midnight when Rescue Center called the helicopter with instructions to return to Danang. The message was not well received by the Jolly Green Giant's crew. The copilot, Captain Ralph Brower, said, "Hell, we're airborne and hot to trot." Staff Sergeant Eugene L. Clay and Sergeant Larry W. Maysey agreed. It was unanimous. The pilot and rescue crew commander, Captain Gerald O. Young, called the center back, requesting permission to continue the mission. Finally he received word that his chopper could accompany the rescue force as a backup to the primary recovery helicopter.

Captain Young's bird was part of a team that included another HH-3E, a C-130 flareship, and three US Army helicopter gunships. The armada was headed toward Khe Sanh, a small city in the northwesternmost corner of South Vietnam.

That afternoon in the jungles to the southeast of Khe Sanh, a North Vietnamese Battalion had ambushed a small US-South Vietnamese reconnaissance team. They then shot down two helicopters attempting to rescue the survivors. As evening fell, the enemy felt certain that there would be another rescue attempt either that night or early the next morning. With the survivors as bait, they would lure the rescue force into the deadly "flak trap" again.

Shortly after midnight on the 9th of November, the sounds of approaching aircraft brought feelings of hope to the survivors and anticipation to the North Vietnamese gunners. Flares from the C-130 cut through the darkness, illuminating the hillsides below. Once again the rescue effort was underway.

Low clouds and poor visibility forced the choppers to operate within range of the hostile guns, and the enemy opened fire on the gunships. Reacting swiftly, the small helicopters evaded the withering fire and answered with a stream of rockets and machine gun bullets. The big Jollys hovered nearby, waiting for a chance to make the pickup. Suddenly, the ground fire ceased.

Like motorcycles preceding a limousine, the gunships escorted the first Jolly Green Giant, strafing the silent enemy positions to protect the defenseless rescue bird. The Jolly settled slowly into place alongside a steep slope when the hillside erupted once more. The gunners fired at close range from atop a nearby ridge, and the hovering helicopter was an easy target in the ghostly flarelight. As three survivors clambered aboard, the Jolly broke out of the hover and wheeled away from the murderous barrage.

Leaking fuel, oil, and hydraulic fluid, the bullet-riddled HH-3 struggled to reach altitude. Her pilot had been forced to withdraw before two wounded Americans and the remaining survivors could be picked up. Captain Young's copilot warned the crippled ship to head for the landing strip at Khe Sanh. The Jolly would never be able to make it back to Danang. Enroute to a successful emergency landing, the pilot advised that rescue attempts should be suspended because of the intense ground fire and the low fuel state of the gunships.

Though they could easily have chosen to escort their sister ship to safety, Gerald Young and his crew decided to stay. This was the very reason that they had volunteered to come as the backup ship. There was still a job to be done.

The crew had a plan. While Captain Young maneuvered the chopper into position, Captain Brower would direct the supporting fire of the gunships. As soon as the Jolly touched down, Sergeant Maysey would alight and lift the wounded survivors to Sergeant Clay. It would be a team effort all the way.

It took a steady hand to hover a helicopter over a flat pad in broad daylight. It would take fantastic skill and discipline to approach the hillside in the middle of the night under a hail of hostile fire. As Brower called out the enemy positions, Young eased the chopper down. He was forced to land with only one main wheel on the slope to prevent the roter blade from contacting the hill. As Sergeant Maysey leaped to the jungle floor, Sergeant Clay covered him with the Jolly's machine gun. Hanging in suspended animation awaiting the survivors, the chopper was hit by the deadly accurate fire of the North Vietnamese.

With the last of the soldiers aboard, Gerald applied full power for takeoff as enemy riflemen appeared in plain sight. They raked the bird with small arms fire and rifle-launched grenades. Suddenly the right engine sparked and exploded, and the blast flipped the HH-3 on its back and sent it cascading down the hillside in flames.

Captain Young hung upside down in the cockpit, his clothing afire. After struggling to kick out the side window and release the seat belt, he fell free and tumbled 100 yards to the bottom of the ravine. Frantically he beat out the flames, but not before suffering second and third degree burns on one-fourth of his body.

One man who had been thrown clear lay unconscious nearby, his foot afire. Young crawled to his side and smothered the flame with his bare hands. Trying to move up the hill to help those who had been trapped in the mangled helicopter, he was driven back down the slope by searing heat and whining bullets. Gerald dragged the unconscious man into the bushes, treated him for shock and then concealed himself in the ravine.

Meanwhile, the rescue effort continued. Two A–1E Sandys arrived in the area at 3:30 a.m. The prop-driven aircraft could not make radio contact with the survivors because rescue beeper signals blocked the emergency channel, making voice transmission impossible. The Sandys circled the triangle of burning helicopters and planned a "first light" rescue effort to begin at dawn. They would fly low and slow over the crash site to attract enemy fire. Fighter bombers and helicopter gunships would then pound the hostile positions while the Sandys escorted Jolly Green Giants in for the pickup. There was no more to be done till daybreak.

As the eastern sky lightened, the Sandys began to troll slowly over the helicopter graveyard. They were elated to see Captain Young emerge from hiding and shoot a signal flare. Gerald had been trying to warn them that the North Vietnamese would probably use him as bait for their flak trap, but the beepers continued to prevent radio contact. Sensing a trap, the lead Sandy made 40 low passes, but the enemy did not respond. Had they pulled out before dawn? There was no way to be sure. At 7 a.m., the Sandys were replaced by another pair of A–1Es, and they returned to base for fuel.

For two hours there had been no opposition, and the Sandy pilots had located five survivors near one of the wrecked birds. They escorted several Army and Vietnamese Air Force helicopters in for a successful pickup. Low on fuel, the choppers departed. Things had gone smoothly since daybreak. No flak traps and no exploding choppers.

Circling back to the downed rescue ship, the Sandys again located

Captain Young and the unconscious survivor. They also spotted North Vietnamese troops moving back into the area from the south. Fearing a repetition of the same nightmarish scenario, the rescue forces could not risk bringing a nearby Jolly down for a rescue attempt.

The A–1s dueled with the ground gunners inflicting heavy losses. Sandy lead laid down a smokescreen between the enemy and the survivors and led the rescue choppers in from the north. Flanking the smokescreen, the North Vietnamese opened fire again. This time they scored, ripping the lead A–1 with armor-piercing shells and forcing him to depart for a safe area. The wingman laid down another smokescreen to shield Gerald Young and protect the rescue helicopters.

In the jungle below, Gerald hid the wounded man and stole into the underbrush. He would help in the only way he could, by leading the enemy away from the crash site to take the pressure off the rescue force.

The plan worked. The enemy pursued throughout the day. Dazed and nearly in shock, he hid frequently to treat his burns. As North Vietnamese soldiers approached, Young crawled into an open field and soon found that he was moving in circles in the tall elephant grass. Certain that the enemy wanted him to contact the rescue force, he stuck by his decision not to expose the friendly aircraft to another ambush.

In the meantime, the helicopters were finally able to land a rescue party at the crash site. One survivor was rescued and the bodies of the crewmembers were recovered.

Seventeen hours after the crash and six miles from the crash site, Gerald Young finally escaped his pursuers. Only then was he able to signal a friendly helicopter. The ordeal was over.

November 26, 1968

Just before noon on 26 November 1968, a transport helicopter inserted a Special Forces team into hostile territory in the western highlands of South Vietnam. The UH–1F chopper was manned by Lieutenant James P. Fleming, aircraft commander; Major Paul E. McClellan, copilot; and the gunners, Staff Sergeant Fred J. Cook and Sergeant Paul R. Johnson.

Four hours later the reconnaissance team made contact with the enemy. Their leader, Lieutenant Randolph C. Harrison, sent out a radio call for gunship fire support, but the green berets quickly realized that they were hopelessly outnumbered and called again for immediate evacuation.

Overhead, an Air Force FAC responded to the urgent request. He found the six men pinned down along a river bank and under intense fire from heavy machine guns and automatic weapons.

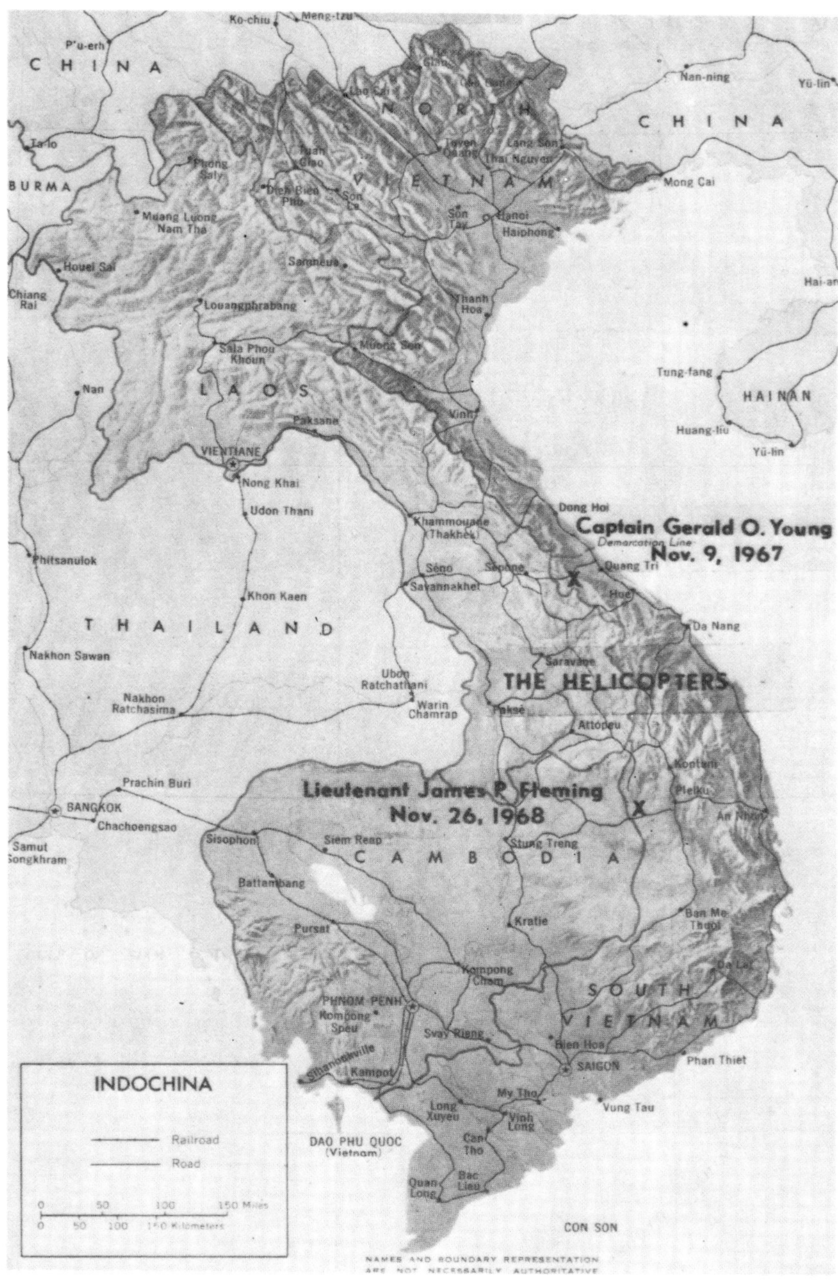

Captain Gerald O. Young
Nov. 9, 1967
Demarcation Line
THE HELICOPTERS
Lieutenant James P. Fleming
Nov. 26, 1968
INDOCHINA
Railroad
Road
0 50 100 150 Miles
0 50 100 150 Kilometers
NAMES AND BOUNDARY REPRESENTATION
ARE NOT NECESSARILY AUTHORITATIVE
CHINA
NORTH VIETNAM
LAOS
THAILAND
CAMBODIA
SOUTH VIETNAM
BURMA
HAINAN
Ko-chiu
Meng-tzu
P'u-erh
Nan-ning
Yü-lin
Mong Cai
Hanoi
Haiphong
Son Tay
Dien Bien Phu
Muang Luong Nam Tha
Houei Sai
Chiang Rai
Louangphrabang
Sala Phou Khoun
Samneua
Thanh Hoa
Vinh
Nan
Paksane
VIENTIANE
Nong Khai
Udon Thani
Tung-fang
Huang-liu
Dong Hoi
Quang Tri
Hue
Da Nang
Phitsanulok
Khon Kaen
Sepone
Savannakhet
Seno
Nakhon Sawan
Nakhon Ratchasima
Ubon Ratchathani
Warin Chamrap
Saravane
Pakse
Attopeu
Kontum
Pleiku
Prachin Buri
BANGKOK
Chachoengsao
Samut Songkhram
Sisophon
Siem Reap
Stung Treng
Battambang
Pursat
Kratie
Ban Me Thuot
Da Lat
Kompong Cham
PHNOM PENH
Kompong Speu
Svay Rieng
Bien Hoa
SAIGON
Phan Thiet
Kampot
My Tho
Vung Tau
Long Xuyen
Vinh Long
Can Tho
Bac Lieu
Quan Long
DAO PHU QUOC
(Vietnam)
CON SON

The FAC, Major Charles E. Anonsen, spotted a clearing in the jungle 100 yards from the green berets and a second, much smaller, clearing within 25 yards. He doubted whether a chopper could land in the second clearing, but the question was academic because the beleaguered Americans were trapped in the dense undergrowth and unable to move toward either one.

Meanwhile, a flight of three transport and two gunship helicopters had also heard the call. The five choppers were enroute to a refueling stop but quickly changed course and headed for the riverbank. Lieutenant Fleming flew the second transport bird.

Major Anonsen briefed the arriving helicopters and asked the green berets to pop a smoke grenade. The red smoke filtering up through the foliage pinpointed the position of the friendly soldiers.

The jungle on three sides of the Americans came alive as the two gunships sent a stream of fire slanting earthward and the enemy instantly answered back. The airborne gunners strained to spot the hostile machine guns as Major Leonard Gonzales and Captain David Miller wheeled their UH–1s above the river.

The gunship crews located the guns 200 yards south of the green berets and ripped the positions with high explosive rockets, destroying two of the heavy weapons. But the North Vietnamese had also found the range and laced Captain Miller's aircraft with machinegun fire.

Despite a rapid loss of oil pressure, Miller's crippled craft made two more firing passes before being riddled by a second accurate burst. Dave Miller knew he was done as he pulled up and out of the fight and headed northeast. As the bird lost power, he steered it to a safe landing in a clearing across the river, performing what Major Anonsen would later call "a beautiful autorotation."

Now the first transport helicopter commanded by Major Dale L. Eppinger swung into action. While the stricken gunship settled into the emergency landing, Eppinger maneuvered his UH–1 to follow closely behind. He touched down alongside the downed bird and instantly Captain Miller and his crew climbed aboard. Low on fuel, the transport bird wheeled away to the forward base at Duc Co.

Within minutes, Miller's abandoned chopper was ripped by enemy fire and destroyed. A second helicopter was forced to depart because of low fuel and only the FAC, one gunship, and one transport bird remained.

The FAC radioed the green berets to move to the small clearing while Lieutenant Fleming descended toward the river. Major Gonzales forced the enemy gunners to keep their heads down as he made multiple passes with guns blazing to cover Jim Fleming's approach.

At treetop height, Jim realized that the clearing was too small and overgrown for a landing, and he headed instead for the nearby riverbank. Perhaps he could hover just above the shoreline with his landing skids bumping the bank and his tail boom extended out over the water. That's exactly what Jim did, performing a feat of unbelievable flying skill as his crew searched frantically for the recon team.

They were nowhere in sight and the team's radioman could barely be heard above the chatter of the hostile guns. Finally, the message came through. The team could not make it to the pickup point.

Fleming's bird was an inviting target as he backed out over the river through a hail of bullets. His gunners, Sergeants Cook and Johnson, answered back, raking the concealed emplacements with M–60 machine gun fire. Major Gonzales said later, "It was a sheer miracle that he wasn't shot down on the takeoff."

Gonzales was nearly out of ammunition, and both he and Jim Fleming were critically low on fuel. If the rescue force withdrew, the American soldiers were doomed. With their backs to the river, the green berets hastily ringed their position with Claymore mines and hoped for a miracle.

Overhead Jim prepared for one last-ditch attempt. He recalls, "The first time we went in I wasn't really conscious of the danger. You know, it was what we had been trained to do. And so we did it. But then I guess it all got to me. Watching Miller getting shot down, the heaviest hostile fire I'd ever seen. . . . Frankly, I was scared to death!"

Nevertheless, Jim let down to the river for the second time, dropping below the bank to partially shield the UH–1 from the deadly barrage. But this time the North Vietnamese knew precisely where he was headed and concentrated their fire on the pickup point, strafing the chopper from all sides.

By now, the six Special Forces men had been under siege for an hour, and the enemy began to move in for the kill. Jim witnessed a grisly scene as the North Vietnamese reached the string of mines and one enemy soldier was blown into the air. The green berets killed three attackers who had advanced to within ten yards of the landing zone, then turned their backs on death and desperately dashed for the helicopter.

In the hovering UH–1, Sergeant Cook fired at the advancing foe while Sergeant Johnson tried in vain to clear a jammed gun. As the team reached the rope ladder, Cook continued firing with one hand, while pulling the soldiers aboard with the other. "Sergeant Cook is about 5 feet 7 and weighs not much more than 120 pounds," Jim Fleming said later. "But those Special Forces boys, some of whom were 200 pounds or more, said that Cook literally lifted them into the helicopter with one hand!"

Jim struggled to hold his craft steady while it rocked and bounced as the green berets climbed aboard. Sergeant Johnson helped Cook drag the last man in as the ship backed out from the bank and sped downriver, the rope ladder dragging in the water.

Overhead Major Gonzales, who had been supporting Lieutenant Fleming throughout, ran out of ammunition at the very moment that the team climbed to safety. He had strafed within five yards of the friendly soldiers to screen them from the enemy.

It was only as the two choppers whirled eastward to Duc Co with fuel tanks nearly dry that Jim Fleming and Paul McClellan noticed the bullet holes in the windshield. Neither could remember being hit and neither cared to dwell on the fact that they had missed death by inches.

Chapter V. The Cargo Gunships

The Job

Hauling supplies and personnel is not the most glamorous job in peace or war. But Air Force transport crews in Southeast Asia provided the last link in a supply chain that stretched from the States across the Pacific to the combat zone. Flying around the clock, the C–123 and C–130 aircraft carried troops, ammunition, fuel, spare parts, supplies, food, and mail from the major ports in Vietnam to smaller bases throughout the country.

Aircraft response was dramatically demonstrated during the resupply of isolated Army and Marine camps under siege by the Vietcong. Often risking their lives by flying through areas of hostile groundfire, the transport crews delivered the vital supplies that allowed American soldiers to repel enemy attacks. The big cargo birds could land on a short dirt strip, offload with engines running, and take off in a few minutes, carrying the wounded to safety. If groundfire was so intense that landing was impossible, the crew could airdrop supplies by parachute to the embattled outpost. The cargo ships could also drop Army paratroopers into an objective area for a rapid assault on the elusive enemy.

The development of gunships was spurred by the unique requirements of a jungle war. Machine guns were mounted on cargo aircraft and the birds were assigned the mission of denying the Vietcong the cover of night. The gunships were ideally suited for areas where the enemy's antiaircraft defenses were light. The slow-moving transports could stay airborne longer and carry more ammunition than the high-speed fighters.

The gunships orbited above a suspected enemy location and responded immediately to a request from friendly ground forces for firepower support. The loadmaster dropped flares to light the countryside exposing the enemy, while the pilot fired a withering stream of bullets with deadly accuracy. Tracer ammunition sent neon-like

C–123 Aircraft

AC–47 Aircraft

streams of light toward the target, allowing the pilot to adjust his aim point as he banked and turned the aircraft.

Later in the war, more sophisticated gunships used infrared radar to seek out ground targets. These aircraft strafed enemy trucks with pinpoint precision, disrupting the flow of supplies that moved each night along the Ho Chi Minh trail. Transport crews assigned to gunship duty relished the long-awaited opportunity to shoot back at the Vietcong.

The Aircraft

The Fairchild-Hiller built C–123 Provider carried 60 troops or 12 tons of cargo. Pallets and vehicles were rapidly loaded through a tail ramp in the aft fuselage, and paratroopers jumped from smaller doors on either side of the aircraft. With a full payload, the Provider weighed over 30 tons.

Two small jets were added to later models of the twin-engine, prop-driven bird for improved takeoff performance and load-carrying capability. The jets were fired up for takeoff, allowing a short ground roll and a quicker climb to altitude. The steep climbout minimized the three-man crew's exposure to groundfire.

The Providers in Vietnam were painted with a camouflage design to give the enemy gunner less time to aim and fire at the cargo ships.

Flying at a top speed of 230 miles per hour, the C–123 often flew many sorties in a single day, leapfrogging from one dirt strip to the next to supply remote Army outposts.

****

The C–47 Skytrain or Gooney Bird is the military version of the DC–3 airliner, which first flew in 1935. More than 10,000 DC–3 type airplanes have been manufactured. The Gooney Bird was the backbone of troop-carrier commands in all theaters of operations during World War II, and it was used extensively in Korea.

Seeing its third war, in Vietnam, the C–47 was used for intratheater airlift by the Air Forces of the United States and South Vietnam. A modified version was employed for psychological warfare, including leaflet drops and loudspeaker broadcasts.

In November 1965, a new model was introduced in Vietnam. The venerable Gooney Bird became a tactical attack aircraft, the AC–47 Dragonship. Christened originally as "Puff the Magic Dragon," the AC–47 had three 7.62 millimeter mini-guns jutting from two windows and the cargo door. The 6,000 rounds-a-minute mini-guns were fired by the pilot, who aimed through a side window sight while turning the aircraft in a steep, left bank.

Lt. Col. Joe M. Jackson

A1C John L. Levitow

The Dragonship was used primarily for night airborne alert, dropping flares and providing firepower for outposts or friendly troops under attack by insurgent forces.

The Men

Joe M. Jackson was born on March 14, 1923, in Newnan, Georgia. He enlisted in the Army Air Corps in 1941 and sought duty as an aircraft mechanic. After serving as a crew chief in a B–25 bomber unit, Sergeant Jackson began pilot training, earning his wings and a commission in 1943. He flew 107 fighter missions in Korea and won the Distinguished Flying Cross.

Colonel Jackson was one of the first Air Force pilots to fly the high-altitude U–2 reconnaissance plane. In the early 1960s he served on the staff at Strategic Air Command Headquarters and drew up the operations plans for aerial reconnaissance of Cuba during the missile crisis.

After 20 years as a fighter pilot, Colonel Jackson was assigned to transport duty. The 45-year-old officer won the Medal of Honor in Vietnam in 1968 and flew 296 sorties during his combat tour.

****

John L. Levitow was born in Hartford, Connecticut, on November 1, 1945, and grew up in nearby Glastonbury. He completed Air Force basic training in 1966, and reported to McGuire AFB, New Jersey.

At McGuire, Airman Levitow served as a powerline specialist until he crosstrained into flight duty, becoming an aircraft loadmaster.

In July 1968, he reported for service in Vietnam and flew 180 combat sorties before the Medal of Honor mission in February 1969. The 23-year-old also earned the Air Medal with seven oak leaf clusters, the Bronze Star, and the Purple Heart. John Levitow is the youngest and lowest ranking Air Force enlisted man to win the Medal of Honor.

May 12, 1968

Not many pilots looked forward to a flight check. As inevitable as desk jobs and remote assignments, flight checks were something you learned to live with. Twice a year the Air Force wanted to be reassured that you still had the skills and knowledge to accomplish the mission effectively and safely. It mattered little if you were a colonel or a lieutenant, if you'd flown the flight check profile many times before, or if the flight examiner was your best friend. You knew that you were expected to do a first-rate job and that the examiner would write an objective report on your performance. Not really something to get sweaty palms over, but never taken lightly either. Check rides in a combat zone? Of course. The Air Force's mission was to fly and fight and do them professionally.

On May 12, 1968, C–123 number 542 lined up on the runway at Danang Air Base. The Provider was scheduled to swing north toward the Demilitarized Zone and back down the coast toward Chu Lai, stopping enroute to resupply several outposts. The cargo bird could carry a good load and still land and take off from the temporary jungle strips.

Lieutenant Colonel Joe M. Jackson was at the controls and Major Jesse Campbell was the flight examiner in the right seat. Technical Sergeant Edward M. Trejo and Staff Sergeant Manson L. Grubbs rounded out 542's crew.

As he guided the Provider into the air and retracted the gear and flaps, Joe Jackson remembered that it was Mother's Day. But thoughts of family must wait. He had supplies to deliver and a check ride to pass.

The weather along the coast was good and the mission went well. Joe had successfully completed all flight-check requirements when the crew got an unexpected message to return to home base.

Meanwhile, 45 miles to the southwest of Danang, near the Laotian border, a massive airlift operation was underway at Kham Duc. A steady stream of C–123s and C–130s shuttled into the isolated Special Forces camp to evacuate 1,000 friendly troops. Vastly outnumbered, they had been under siege by a communist force for three days. Now the outpost was in danger of being overrun.

Lieutenant Colonel Jackson and his crew were briefed at Danang on the emergency rescue operation, and they were airborne again in less than an hour, heading southwest toward Kham Duc. As they flew inland the weather deteriorated, but the C–123 entered a holding pattern south of the camp at 3:30 p.m.

The evacuation was a hectic operation. An airborne command post controlled the flow of cargo planes into the short strip that lay unprotected on the valley floor. Forward air controllers directed fighter-bombers against Vietcong positions surrounding the runway. As number 542 moved closer to the camp, smoke and flames from exploding ammunition dumps and tracers from enemy weapons were clearly visible, even from an altitude of 9,000 feet.

Joe and his crew relaxed as the radio chatter confirmed that the last suvivors had been rescued. Now the command post directed the fighters to destroy the camp and the enemy with it. But something was wrong. An animated voice on the radio warned that three US airmen had been left behind.

Attempts to contact the three combat controllers failed, and the command post asked the C–123 ahead of number 542 to land and try to pick them up. As the Provider approached the runway, she drew flak like a magnet. The fighters tried to protect the slow-moving bird by strafing the jungles as the enemy opened up with machine guns, mortars, and recoilless rifles. The Americans had snatched 1,000 men from under the Vietcong's nose, and the Cong wanted someone to pay the price.

As the aircraft touched down, she came under intense fire from positions on the edge of the runway. Seeing no chance to locate the three airmen, let along pick them up, the pilot jammed the throttles full forward and prepared for takeoff. Just before liftoff the crew spotted the three combat controllers crouching in a ditch bordering the runway, but it was too late to stop. The C–123 lifted off through a volley of bullets. Low on fuel, she headed for home base.

Joe Jackson had an answer for the question even before it was asked. Would he? "There wasn't any question about it. There wasn't any decision to make. Of course, we would make the attempt." Jesse Campbell radioed, "Roger. Going in."

Technical Sergeant Mort Freedman spoke for the combat controllers, describing how he, Major John Gallagher, and Sergeant Jim Lundie reacted when the last Provider took off, leaving the three-man team behind. "The pilot saw no one left on the ground, so he took off. We figured no one would come back and we had two choices. Either be taken prisoner or fight it out. There was no doubt about it. We had 11 magazines left among us, and we were going to take as many of them with us as we could."

Lieutenant Colonel Jackson called on his fighter-pilot experience and decided to try a new tactic. He knew the Vietcong gunners would expect him to follow the same flight path as the other cargo birds. What if he could take an elevator straight down into the valley?

Nine thousand feet high and rapidly approaching the landing area, he pointed 542's nose down in a steep dive. The book said you didn't fly transports this way. But the guy who wrote the book had never been shot at. Joe recalls, "I had two problems, the second stemming from the first. One was to avoid reaching 'blow up' speed, where the flaps, which were in full down position for the dive, are blown back up to neutral. If this happened, we would pick up even more speed, leading to problem two, the danger of overshooting the runway."

Taken by surprise, the enemy gunners reacted in time to open fire as the diving Provider neared the strip. Joe coaxed her nose up, breaking the dizzying descent just above the treetops, one quarter of a mile from the end of the runway. He barely had time to set up a landing attitude as the Provider settled toward the threshold.

The debris-littered runway looked like an obstacle course. Just 2,200 feet from the touchdown point a burning helicopter blocked the way. He knew he would have to stop in a hurry, but Joe Jackson decided against using reverse thrust to slow the bird. Reversing the engines would automatically shut off the two jets that would be needed for a minimum-run takeoff. He stood on the brakes like no Indianapolis driver ever had.

Number 542 skidded to a stop just before reaching the gutted helicopter. Three men scrambled from the ditch, reaching the airplane as Sergeant Grubbs lowered the rear door. He and Sergeant Trejo pulled them aboard.

In the meantime, Major Campbell spotted a 122-millimeter rocket shell, and the two pilots watched in horror as it came to rest just 25 feet in front of the nose. Luck was still on their side. The deadly projectile did not explode.

Joe taxied around the shell and rammed the throttles to the firewall. "We hadn't been out of that spot ten seconds when mortars started dropping directly on it," he remembers. "That was a real thriller. I figured they just got zeroed in on us, and that the time of flight of the mortar shells was about ten seconds longer than the time we sat there taking the men aboard." Dodging shell craters, 542 accelerated down the runway.

Just ahead tracers illuminated a murderous crossfire, but there was no turning back. "We were scared to death," Jackson said.

The ship broke ground, slowly picking up speed and climbing toward intense fire from the far end of the runway. Nothing to do now but press on, wishing that they could take the same elevator out of there. At last Kham Duc was behind them.

Number 542, a peaceful cargo bird once more, landed at Danang at 5:30 p.m. with her four-man crew and three passengers. Miraculously, she had not taken one hit! "I will never understand that," is Lieutenant Colonel Jackson's comment. "And to think, I only flew that day because it seemed like a good time to get a needed flight check!"

Sergeant Freedman added a simple postscript. "If they hadn't gone

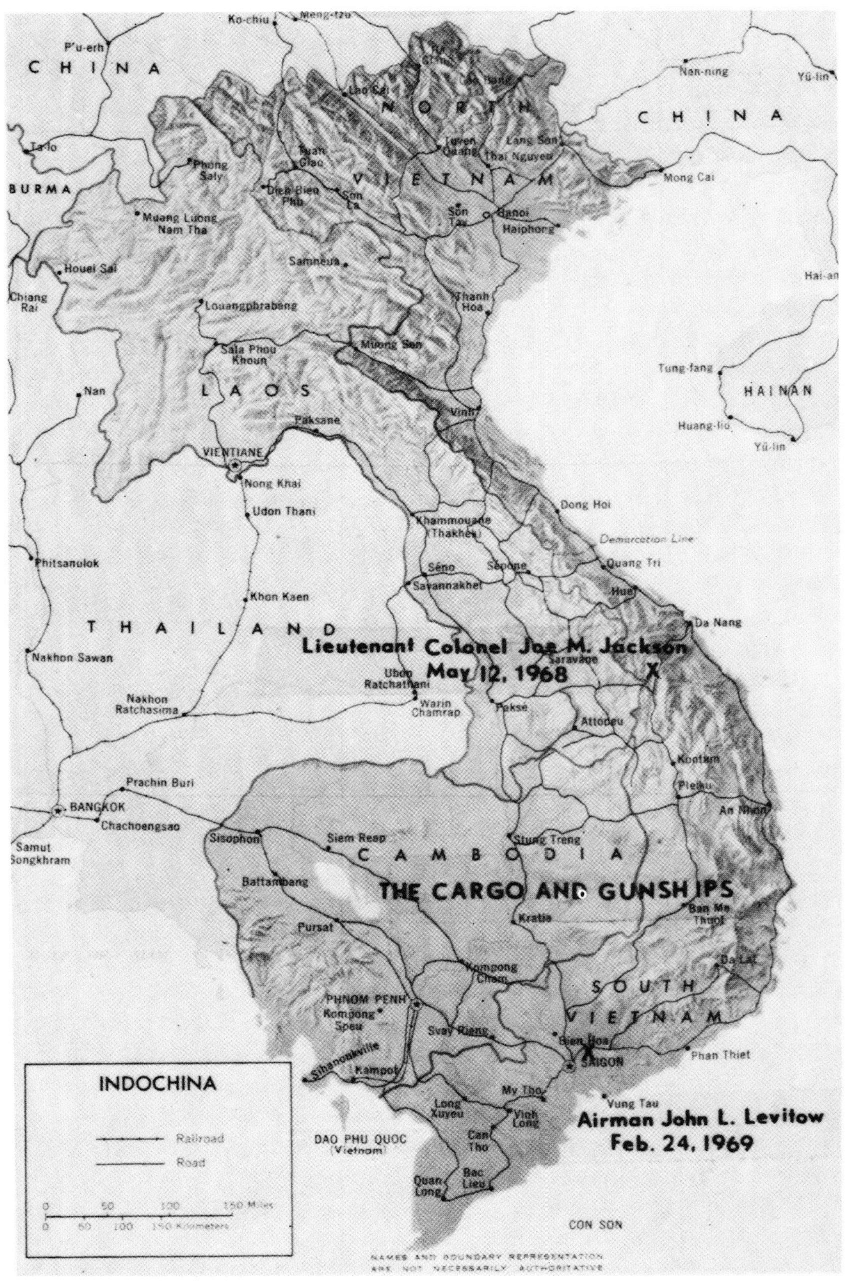

INDOCHINA
Railroad
Road
0 50 100 150 Miles
0 50 100 150 Kilometers
CHINA
BURMA
NORTH VIETNAM
LAOS
THAILAND
CAMBODIA
SOUTH VIETNAM
HAINAN
Ko-chiu
Meng-tzu
P'u-erh
Nan-ning
Yü-lin
Lao Cai
Cao Bang
Tuyen Quang
Lang Son
Thai Nguyen
Mong Cai
Ta-lo
Phong Saly
Dien Bien Phu
Son La
Son Tay
Hanoi
Haiphong
Muang Luong Nam Tha
Houei Sai
Samneua
Chiang Rai
Louangphrabang
Thanh Hoa
Muong Sen
Sala Phou Khoun
Nan
Vinh
Paksane
Tung-fang
Huang-liu
VIENTIANE
Nong Khai
Udon Thani
Dong Hoi
Khammouane (Thakhek)
Demarcation Line
Phitsanulok
Séno
Sepone
Quang Tri
Savannakhet
Hue
Khon Kaen
Da Nang
Lieutenant Colonel Joe M. Jackson
May 12, 1968
X
Nakhon Sawan
Saravane
Ubon Ratchathani
Warin Chamrap
Nakhon Ratchasima
Pakse
Attopeu
Kontum
Pleiku
Prachin Buri
BANGKOK
Chachoengsao
An Nhon
Samut Songkhram
Sisophon
Siem Reap
Stung Treng
Battambang
THE CARGO AND GUNSHIPS
Kratie
Ban Me Thuot
Pursat
Da Lat
Kompong Cham
PHNOM PENH
Kompong Speu
Svay Rieng
Bien Hoa
X
SAIGON
Phan Thiet
Sihanoukville
Kampot
My Tho
Vung Tau
Long Xuyen
Vinh Long
Airman John L. Levitow
Feb. 24, 1969
DAO PHU QUOC (Vietnam)
Can Tho
Bac Lieu
Quan Long
CON SON
NAMES AND BOUNDARY REPRESENTATION ARE NOT NECESSARILY AUTHORITATIVE

in, there is no doubt that we would have been killed or captured." Mother's Day 1968, Vietnamese style, was over.

February 24, 1969

On the evening of 24 February 1969, an AC–47 with the call sign "Spooky 71" lifted off the runway at Bien Hoa Air Base. As the Gooney Bird climbed into the clear night sky, her eight-man crew prepared for a long combat air patrol mission in the Saigon area. In the cargo compartment, the crew's loadmaster, Airman First Class John L. Levitow, was airborne on his 180th combat mission.

One of John's responsibilities on the gunship was handling the Mark 24 flares. He would set the ejection and ignition controls and pass the flare to the gunner, Airman Ellis C. Owen, who attached it to a lanyard. On the pilot's command, Owen would simultaneously pull the safety pin and toss the flare through the open cargo door.

The Mark 24 looked innocent enough. It was a three-foot-long metal tube weighing 27 pounds. Ten seconds after release an explosive charge deployed a parachute. In another ten seconds the magnesium flare would ignite, quickly reaching a temperature of 4,000 degrees Fahrenheit and illuminating the countryside with two million candlepower. Drifting slowly beneath its chute, each flare would burn for over a minute.

The Vietcong guerrillas, peasants by day and terrorists by night, were denied the protection of darkness when Spooky was about.

Spooky 71 and her crew had been airborne for 4½ hours when the pilot, Major Ken Carpenter, received word of enemy action around Bien Hoa. As Carpenter wheeled the Gooney Bird back toward its home field, he and his copilot saw muzzle flashes from the perimeter of the Long Binh Army Base below. The Vietcong were busy here, also.

The gunship circled in an orbit centered around the muzzle flashes. In two lightning-quick attacks with mini-guns chattering, she slammed 3,000 rounds of ammunition into the enemy positions. Spooky 71 received an urgent request to remain in the vicinity to provide illumination for friendly ground forces. Obviously, the area around Long Binh was the new hot spot.

Major Carpenter received a second call requesting illumination in an area two miles south of Long Binh. As the aircraft swung to the south, the pilots saw flashes from a heavy mortar barrage ahead. The crew in the cargo compartment followed the sounds of the action. Later, John Levitow recalled, "Every once in a while, you'd hear a muffled noise when a mortar hit. You could hear the engines on the aircraft, the noise of the guns firing and the pilot giving instructions."

Suddenly, Spooky 71 was jarred by a tremendous explosion and bathed in a blinding flash of light. The crew would learn later that a

North Vietnamese Army 82-millimeter mortar shell had landed on top of the right wing and exploded inside the wing frame. The blast raked the fuselage with flying shrapnel.

In the cockpit the pilots struggled to bring the lurching Gooney Bird under control. They had been momentarily blinded, and the navigator, Major William Platt recalls, "Even in the navigation compartment, the flash lit up the inside of the aircraft like daylight. The aircraft veered sharply to the right and down." Though the situation was desperate in the cockpit, it was even worse in the cargo compartment.

Sergeant Edward Fuzie, who was wounded in the back and neck, remembers, "I saw Sergeant Baer, Airman Owen, and Airman Levitow go down right away. Baer was covered with blood."

John Levitow thought one of the mini-guns had exploded. In his words, "But when I was actually hit, the shrapnel felt like a two-by-four, or a large piece of wood which had been struck against my side. It stung me. I really didn't know what it was."

Airman Owen was the first to realize that the Spooky crew was still in mortal danger. "I had the lanyard on one flare hooked up, and my finger was through the safety pin ring. When we were hit, all three of us were thrown to the floor. The flare, my finger still through the safety pin ring, was knocked out of my hand. The safety pin was pulled and the flare rolled on the aircraft floor, fully armed!"

Major Carpenter learned via the intercom that everyone in the back was wounded and a live flare was loose in the plane. In the meantime, John Levitow came to the aid of a fellow crewmember, who was perilously close to the open cargo door. As he dragged his buddy back toward the center of the cabin, John saw the flare.

The canister rolled crazily amidst the ammunition cans which contained over 19,000 rounds of live ammunition. In less than 20 seconds the AC–47 would become a flaming torch, plunging its crews to destruction in the night sky. John had no way of knowing how many seconds remained. The beating the flare had already taken could have damaged the timer, causing ignition before the 20 seconds had elapsed. He was weak from loss of blood and numb from the 40 wounds on his right side. But John knew he was the closest to the flare.

Time and again the smoking tube eluded his grasp as the aircraft pitched and rolled. In desperation, he threw himself on the flare and painfully dragged it toward the cargo door, leaving a trail of blood behind. The seconds ticked by. With a final superhuman effort John heaved the flare through the door. It barely cleared the aircraft before igniting in an incandescent blaze.

Major Carpenter recalls, "I had the aircraft in a 30-degree bank and how Levitow ever managed to get to the flare and throw it out, I'll never know." As he finally brought the ship back to straight and level flight, Major Carpenter headed toward Bien Hoa. He radioed for an ambulance and a medical evacuation helicopter to meet the gunship.

Major Carpenter spoke later about John Levitow and the Gooney Bird. "After the mission I was able to reconstruct what happened by the blood trail left by John. He collapsed after throwing the flare overboard and was evacuated to the base hospital immediately upon landing. In my experience, I have never seen such a courageous act performed under such adverse circumstances. The entire eight-man crew owes their lives to John, and his quick reactions surely saved the aircraft. It was not possible to bail out as we had two seriously injured men aboard, one of them John Levitow. How the plane ever flew back to the base, I'll never know. How a plane with over 3,500 holes in the wings and fuselage stayed airborne defies description. One hole measured 3 feet, 1/4 inches."

Chapter VI. The Prisoners of War

The Job

Nearing the magic 100-mission number that would end his combat tour, the airman prayed that he could continue to dodge the flak and the deadly SAMs that pierced the sky over the heavily-defended targets of North Vietnam. He knew that if he was shot down, a massive rescue effort would be triggered immediately. He realized also that those unlucky enough to be captured would join a group of men who were totally dedicated to resisting their captors.

Most of the prisoners in Vietnam were Air Force and Navy pilots and navigators shot down over the North. The typical Air Force prisoner was a fighter pilot who had survived a bailout from a crippled F–105, F–4, or F–100. Sometimes he was able to evade his pursuers for days, but often his parachute was spotted and he was captured immediately.

The airman knew that the war did not end if he was captured. Bound by the long-standing tradition of the American fighting man and the Code of Conduct, he would be obligated to resist and oppose the enemy while in captivity.

The 247-word Code of Conduct was prescribed by President Eisenhower in 1955. Under the Code, POWs are required to make every effort to escape and aid others to escape. The senior-ranking prisoner is obligated to take command, and all subordinates will obey his lawful orders. Though it is mandatory to give name, rank, service number, and date of birth, American servicemen will evade answering further questions to the utmost of their ability.

Failing to abide by the Geneva convention, the communists resorted to torture and brainwashing, trying to force the Americans to reveal military information or denounce their government. A prisoner, tortured to the breaking point, who responded to the interrogator's questions knew that he was fully responsible for his statements. Upon repatriation, the man's conduct and the circumstances of his captivity would be examined by military authorities.

F–100 Aircraft

F–4 Aircraft

Though unsuccessful, the attempt in 1970 to rescue the POWs in the daring Son Tay prison raid demonstrated to the world that America had not forgotten her bravest sons.

In February 1973 the first POWs were released by the North Vietnamese. By the end of March all surviving prisoners had been repatriated. Navy Lieutenant Commander Everett Alvarez, Jr., who was a captive for eight and one-half years, was the longest held pilot. Sixteen Air Force men were reported to have died in captivity and 324 returned.

In 1973, after almost six years of captivity, Lieutenant Colonel Leo Thorsness was awarded the Medal of Honor for his heroic 1967 mission. Leo described his reaction. "I was proud and humble, but prison taught me there are other things that test a man more than combat. At no time in an airplane did I ever fear. There's a certain security in the cockpit. In prison you are by yourself, and it continues day after day. It is unfortunate that Medals of Honor are not presented under the most trying test of a man's courage, bravery, and capabilities." Leo's statement proved prophetic.

In 1976, President Ford announced that the Medal of Honor would be presented to three former POWs. Colonel George E. Day and Captain Lance P. Sijan were recognized along with Navy Rear Admiral James B. Stockdale for their heroism in captivity.

The Aircraft

The F–105 Thunderchiefs carried the war to the enemy heartland. With aerial refueling, the Thuds ranged far from their bases in Thailand. Before the bombing halt, the 105s struck military targets near Hanoi, and Thunderchief wild weasels attacked the enemy's antiaircraft defenses.

The F–4 Phantoms proved their worth whether striking ground targets with heavy bomb loads or dueling with MIG interceptors in a classic dogfight. With air-to-air missiles and a 20-millimeter cannon at his command, Phantom pilot Captain Richard S. Ritchie shot down five MIGs to become an ace.

The venerable single engine F–100 first flew in 1953. It was the first Air Force fighter to break the sound barrier in level flight. The two-seat model of the Super Sabre was used as a high-speed FAC aircraft in North Vietnam. In South Vietnam, the "Huns" were often scrambled from ground alert to support friendly troops in contact with the enemy.

The Men

George E. Day was born at Sioux City, Iowa, on February 24, 1925.

Enlisting in the Marine Corps in 1942, he served 30 months in the South Pacific during World War II.

Following the war, George returned to civilian life to complete his education. After earning a master's degree, a Juris Doctor, and admission to the South Dakota bar, he was commissioned in the Air National Guard in 1950. The 26-year-old was called to active duty to begin pilot training in 1951.

He served two tours as a fighter-bomber pilot in the Far East during the Korean War. In a later assignment to England, George became the first pilot to survive a "no-parachute" bailout from a burning jet fighter.

In Vietnam, Colonel Day was the first commander of the F–100 fighter squadron that flew high-speed forward-air-control missions in areas where the slow-moving FAC birds could not survive hostile groundfire.

Colonel Day spent over five years as a prisoner of war after he was shot down over North Vietnam in 1967. He was the only POW to escape from the North Vietnamese to be recaptured later by the Vietcong in the south.

The veteran pilot has flown over 5,000 hours in jet fighters. In addition to the Medal of Honor, he has won the Air Force Cross, Silver Star, Distinguished Flying Cross, Air Medal with nine oak leaf clusters, Bronze Star for valor with two clusters, and the Purple Heart with three clusters.

****

Lance P. Sijan was born on April 13, 1942, in Milwaukee, Wisconsin. He graduated from the Air Force Academy and was commissioned in June 1965. After pilot training at Laredo, Texas, Captain Sijan was assigned to jet fighter duty at George Air Force Base, California.

In July 1967 he was assigned to Danang Air Base, Republic of Vietnam. In November, his F–4C Phantom was shot down over North Vietnam. Captain Sijan was declared missing in action until his death in captivity was confirmed.

In addition to the Medal of Honor, he won the Distinguished Flying Cross, the Air Medal with five oak leaf clusters, and the Purple Heart with one cluster.

August 26, 1967–March 14, 1973

On August 26, 1967, Major George E. Day was airborne over North Vietnam on a forward air control mission when his F–100 was hit by enemy groundfire. During ejection from the stricken fighter his right arm was broken in three places and his left knee was badly

Col. George E. Day

Capt. Lance P. Sijan

sprained. He was immediately captured by the North Vietnamese and taken to a prison camp.

Major Day was continually interrogated and tortured, and his injuries were neglected for two days until a medic crudely set his broken arm. Despite the pain of torture, he steadfastly refused to give any information to his captors.

On September 1, feigning a severe back injury, George lulled his guards into relaxing their vigil and slipped out of his ropes to escape into the jungle. During the trek south toward the demilitarized zone, he evaded enemy patrols and survived on a diet of berries and uncooked frogs. On the second night a bomb or rocket detonated nearby, and Major Day was hit in the right leg by the shrapnel. He was bleeding from the nose and ears due to the shock effect of the explosion. To rest and recover from these wounds, George hid in the jungle for two days.

Continuing the nightmarish journey, he met barrages from American artillery as he neared the Ben Hai River, which separated North Vietnam from South Vietnam. With the aid of a float made from a bamboo log, he swam across the river and entered the no man's land called the demilitarized zone. Delirious and disoriented from his injuries, George wandered aimlessly for several days, trying frantically to signal US aircraft. He was not spotted by two FAC pilots who flew directly overhead, and, later, George limped toward two Marine helicopters only to arrive at the landing zone just after the choppers pulled away.

Twelve days after the escape, weakened from exposure, hunger, and his wounds, Major Day was ambushed and captured by the Vietcong. He suffered gunshot wounds to his left hand and thigh while trying to elude his pursuers. George was returned to the original prison camp and brutally punished for his escape attempt.

On a starvation diet, the 170-pound man shrank to 110 pounds. He was refused medical treatment for broken bones, gunshot wounds, and infections. Renewing the pressure to force Major Day to give vital military information, the North Vietnamese beat and tortured him for two days. Finally, he was bound by a rope under his armpits and suspended from a ceiling beam for over two hours until the interrogating officer ordered a guard to twist his mangled right arm, breaking George's wrist.

At this point Major Day appeared to cooperate with his captors, who felt that they had broken him at last. However, facing death if he was discovered, George deliberately gave false answers to their questions, revealing nothing of military significance.

Two months after his Super Sabre had been shot down, Major Day was transferred to a prison camp near the capital city of Hanoi. By this time he was totally incapacitated, with infections in his arms and legs and little feeling in his twisted hands. George could not perform even the simplest tasks for himself, but still he was tortured. Almost unbelievably, his commitment to utterly resist every attempt to gain military intelligence never wavered. By withholding information despite the cost in personal suffering, George Day sought to protect fellow airmen who were still flying missions against the northern strongholds of the enemy. He did not fail.

After five and one-half years of captivity, Colonel George E. Day was released with his comrades in arms, the American prisoners of war, on March 14, 1973.

November 9, 1967–January 22, 1968

On November 9, 1967, Captain Lance P. Sijan began an ordeal that a fighter pilot can never be entirely prepared for. Secure in the familiar cockpit of his F–4C fighter in one instant, he ejected from the crippled machine in the next heartbeat after an accurate burst of groundfire took its toll. In a brief moment of calm, he was swinging in his parachute above the hostile countryside, and after a bone-jarring landing, he was alone in enemy territory near Vinh, North Vietnam. The precise physical skills of the jet pilot were useless now, but courage and resourcefulness were needed more than ever.

Captain Sijan evaded his pursuers for six weeks but paid a high price for his freedom. During this time he suffered serious injuries to his left leg and right hand as well as a brain concussion and severe

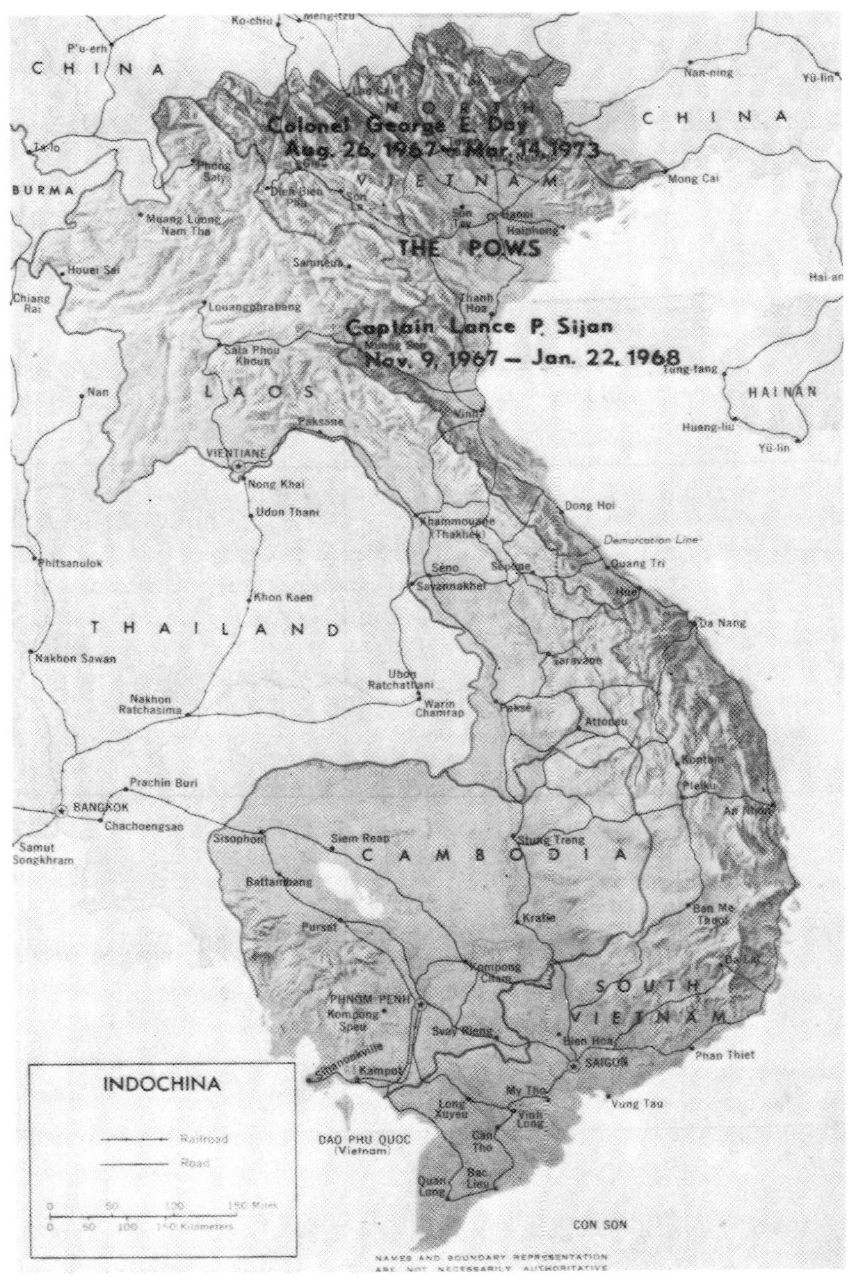
Colonel George E. Day
Aug. 26, 1967 — Mar. 14, 1973
THE P.O.W.S
Captain Lance P. Sijan
Nov. 9, 1967 — Jan. 22, 1968
CHINA
NORTH VIETNAM
CHINA
BURMA
LAOS
THAILAND
CAMBODIA
SOUTH VIETNAM
HAINAN
Ko-chiu
P'u-erh
Nan-ning
Yü-lin
Lao Cai
Phong Saly
Dien Bien Phu
Son Tay
Hanoi
Haiphong
Mong Cai
Muang Luong Nam Tha
Houei Sai
Sam Neua
Chiang Rai
Louangphrabang
Thanh Hoa
Sala Phou Khoun
Muong Sen
Tung-fang
Nan
Vinh
Huang-liu
Yü-lin
Paksane
VIENTIANE
Nong Khai
Udon Thani
Dong Hoi
Khammouane (Thakhek)
Demarcation Line
Phitsanulok
Séno
Sepone
Quang Tri
Savannakhet
Hue
Khon Kaen
Da Nang
Nakhon Sawan
Saravane
Ubon Ratchathani
Nakhon Ratchasima
Warin Chamrap
Pakse
Attopeu
Kontum
Prachin Buri
Pleiku
BANGKOK
Chachoengsao
An Nhon
Samut Songkhram
Sisophon
Siem Reap
Stung Treng
Battambang
Ban Me Thuot
Pursat
Kratie
Kompong Cham
Da Lat
PHNOM PENH
Kompong Speu
Svay Rieng
Bien Hoa
Phan Thiet
Sihanoukville
Kampot
SAIGON
My Tho
Vung Tau
Long Xuyen
Vinh Long
Can Tho
DAO PHU QUOC (Vietnam)
Bac Lieu
Quan Long
CON SON
INDOCHINA
Railroad
Road
0 50 100 150 Miles
0 50 100 150 Kilometers
NAMES AND BOUNDARY REPRESENTATION ARE NOT NECESSARILY AUTHORITATIVE

lacerations. Because of shock and weight loss, Lance was emaciated to a state where every bone showed through his weakened body.

Finally, around Christmas, he was captured by North Vietnamese soldiers and taken to a holding camp. However, Lance found an opportunity, and despite his crippling injuries, he overpowered a guard, knocked him unconscious, and escaped. Again a fugitive, he traveled for two kilometers before being recaptured several hours later and taken to another enroute camp.

After solitary confinement, Captain Sijan was subjected to long interrogations while being tortured for information. Somehow Lance found the strength to resist, and he continually distracted his captors, refusing to tell them anything except name, rank, and serial number.

On January 6, 1968, the North Vietnamese prepared to move some prisoners, and their commander detailed Lieutenant Colonel Robert Craner to care for Captain Sijan. By then, Lance's physical condition had deteriorated to a point where he could neither stand nor sit erect without help.

The next day the two Americans boarded a truck for the long, punishing trip to Hanoi. During the jolting ride, Colonel Craner often feared that Lance had died, but each time he regained consciousness and declared that he was doing all right. Unbelievably, Lance never complained about the battering and, in fact, talked about escape several times, saying that he was ready for another try.

Captain Sijan was taken to Hoa Lo Prison, where he was kept in the section that the American airmen called Vegas. His wounds were not treated, and Lance was able to take only a few spoonfuls of food each day. He grew steadily weaker but requested aid only to put his body in a sitting position so he could exercise his slack muscles in preparation for another escape. Because his broken leg would not support him, Lance had dragged himself backward on his hips during his flight through the jungle. As a result, both hipbones now jutted through his skin and exercise was excruciatingly painful.

His condition aggravated by the poor living conditions, inadequate diet and clothing, Captain Sijan contracted pneumonia on January 18. Because the fluid in his air passages would have strangled him, he could not lie down, and on the night of January 21, the North Vietnamese removed Lance from his cell. The next day they reported that he had died.

Till the end the indomitable airman had resisted the enemy, never complaining about his physical deterioration and eagerly anticipating another chance to escape.

Postscript

In many ways the heroism of the USAF's 12 Medal of Honor winners in Vietnam was unprecedented. These men seldom flew in massive formations of aircraft like World War II heroes who manned the bomber armadas that pounded Hitler's Germany. Nor can they be compared to the fighter aces of past wars whose bravery and skill were tested in the unforgiving arena of air combat. The character of the Vietnam heroes springs instead from the nature of a unique air war and their unique response to its challenge.

In Vietnam, the enemy was clever and dedicated. He often chose to operate in small insurgent bands, using hit-and-run and terrorist tactics. The Vietcong soldier could quickly blend into the local population to become a peasant by day and a guerrilla by night. His hiding places could often be found only by the FAC flying above the jungle in his slow-moving Bird Dog or Bronco.

North Vietnam was supplied with military equipment by her communist allies, and an efficient transportation system funneled these supplies south along the Ho Chi Minh Trail. The communist war machine was protected by defenses that became increasingly more formidable as the war progressed.

The North Vietnamese leaders were politically astute. Seldom were they seen as aggressors in the eyes of the world. Nurturing sympathy for their small nation, the communists provoked a negative reaction against the "imperialism" of the United States. Though they suffered setbacks and delays to their master plan for the takeover of South Vietnam, the North Vietnamese seldom lost sight of this goal.

To fight such an enemy in the Indochina rainforests or the northern industrial areas required that air power be flexible, well-coordinated, and responsive. So it was that WW II vintage C–47s and A–1s flew in the same sky with F–4s and B–52s. Gooney Bird, Skyraider, Phantom and Stratofortress. Each was employed in a role that maximized its special capabilities. Of the ten aircraft flown by the Medal of Honor winners, seven were "slow movers." The FAC, the helicopter pilot, and the transport pilot were as effective as the jet jockey in this war.

So it was that aircraft of the Air Force, Army, Navy, Marine Corps, and the Vietnamese Air Force worked together to get the job done. During the Medal of Honor mission that ultimately cost Captain Steve Bennett his life, he flew with a Marine Corps observer in his back seat. Steve controlled a flight of Navy fighter-bombers and then answered an emergency call to help South Vietnamese ground troops. Such coordination of the air effort was an every day occurrence in Vietnam.

So it was that at 3:00 a.m. on a dark, rainy night, fighter pilots on alert in South Vietnam slept fitfully with their boots on. In minutes after the scramble order came, they would be wide awake at 20,000 feet, streaking toward a target in the southern delta or the northern mountains.

Often the airman in Vietnam was more concerned with saving lives than taking them. President Lyndon B. Johnson made the following remarks at Major Fisher's presentation ceremony:

> I should like to point out that his desire to save lives instead of taking lives is not just confined to Major Fisher. It is rather, I think, typical of all our men in Vietnam. It is particularly true of those who serve with Major Fisher in the most difficult air war in the history of the United States. . . . Like Major Fisher, all of these airmen have accepted an extra risk. . . . These men are conducting the most careful and the most self-limited air war in history. They are trying to apply the maximum amount of pressure with the minimum amount of danger to our own people.

Four of the 12 heroes saved the lives of fellow Americans by daring rescues in the face of overwhelming odds in the enemy's favor. Two heroes saved their fellow crewmembers, while two others risked death to protect an Army unit and a downed airman.The courage of the two prisoners of war grew largely from their fierce desire to deny the North Vietnamese military information about their comrades-in-arms.

Concern for saving lives did not stop with our own people. Strict rules of engagement that required target clearance from high command authority, insured that civilian casualties were minimized throughout the conflict. In the north, in the face of heavy defensive fire, USAF fighter-bombers struck military targets with surgical precision, leaving nearby population centers untouched.

The 12 men number themselves among the 60 USAF Medal of Honor winners of all wars and the 236 men of all services who won the Medal in Vietnam. The stories speak eloquently for the heroes themselves. Though it is interesting to note that their average age was 34 and that seven of the eleven officers began their military careers as enlisted men or aviation cadets, attempts to find a common denominator for bravery prove futile. The single fact that each man rose to meet the challenge in his own way remains. Their courage is an example to all airmen who follow.

Former Chief of Staff General John P. McConnell describes the vital relationship between the character of the man and success in war:

> In my opinion, success in battle will never depend solely on numbers of men or power of weapons, regardless of the dimensions of the war—whether it be a limited war within the confines of a small country like Vietnam or an unlimited war fought on a global battlefield. Ultimately, all weapons come under the control of men, and the knowledge, determination, and courage of those men will govern how well those weapons will be used.

Appendix A. United States Air Force Medal of Honor Winners 1918–1952

(Alphabetically by wars and rank at time of action)

World War I—1918

Bleckley, 2d Lt. Erwin R.*
Gottler, 2d Lt. Harold E.*
Luke, 2d Lt. Frank, Jr.*
Rickenbacker, Capt. Edward V.

Peacetime Award—1927

Lindbergh, Capt. Charles A.

World War II—1942 to 1945

Baker, Lt. Col. Addison E.*
Bong, Maj. Richard I.
Carswell, Maj. Horace S., Jr.*
Castle, Brig. Gen. Frederick W.*
Cheli, Maj. Ralph*
Craw, Col. Demas T.*
Doolittle, Lt. Col. James H.
Erwin, SSgt. Henry E.
Femoyer, 2d Lt. Robert E.*
Gott, 1st Lt. Donald J.*
Hamilton, Maj. Pierpont M.
Howard, Maj. James H.
Hughes, 2d Lt. Lloyd H.*
Jerstad, Maj. John L.*
Johnson, Col. Leon W.
Kane, Col. John R.
Kearby, Col. Neel E.*
Kingsley, 2d Lt. David R.*
Knight, 1st Lt. Raymond L.*
Lawley, 1st Lt. William R., Jr.*
Lindsey, Capt. Darrell R.*
Mathies, SSgt. Archibald*
Mathis, 1st Lt. Jack W.*
McGuire, Maj. Thomas B., Jr.*
Metzger, 2d Lt. William E., Jr.*
Michael, 1st Lt. Edward S.
Morgan, F/O John C.
Pease, Capt. Harl, Jr.*
Pucket, 1st Lt. Donald D.*
Sarnoski, 2d Lt. Joseph R.*
Shomo, Capt. William A.
Smith, SSgt. Maynard H.
Truemper, 2d Lt. Walter E.*
Vance, Lt. Col. Leon R.
Vosler, TSgt. Forrest L.
Walker, Brig. Gen. Kenneth*
Wilkins, Maj. Raymond H.*
Zeamer, Capt. Jay, Jr.*

*Posthumous award.

Peacetime Award—1946

Mitchell, Col. William*

Korea—1950 to 1952

Davis, Lt. Col. George A., Jr.*
Loring, Maj. Charles J., Jr.*
Sebille, Maj. Louis J.*
Walmsley, Capt. John S., Jr.*

---

* Posthumous Award.

Appendix B. United States Air Force Medal of Honor Winners in Vietnam

Name and Rank at Time of Action	Date of Act and Age	Type of Aircraft	Home State
Bennett, Capt. Steven L.*	Jun 29, 1972/ 26	OV–10	Louisiana
Day, Maj. George E.***	Aug 26, 1967/ 42	F–100	Iowa
Dethlefsen, Maj. Merlyn H.	Mar 10, 1967/ 32	F–105	Iowa
Fisher, Maj. Bernard F.	Mar 10, 1966/ 39	A–1	Idaho
Fleming, 1st Lt. James P.	Nov 26, 1968/ 25	UH–1	Washington
Jackson, Lt. Col. Joe M.	May 12, 1969/ 45	C–123	Georgia
Jones, Lt. Col. William A. III**	Sep 1, 1968/ 46	A–1	Virginia
Levitow, A1C John L.	Feb 24, 1969/ 23	AC–47	Connecticut
Sijan, Capt. Lance P.** ***	Nov 9, 1967/ 25	F–4	Wisconsin
Thorsness, Maj. Leo K.	Apr 19, 1967/ 34	F–105	South Dakota
Wilbanks, Capt. Hilliard A.*	Feb 24, 1967/ 33	O–1	Georgia
Young, Capt. Gerald O.	Nov 9, 1967/ 37	HH–3	Illinois

* Posthumous Award, killed in action.

** Posthumous Award, died before presentation.

*** Award for Heroism as a Prisoner of War.

VALOR

Appendix C. Medal of Honor Citations

Steven L. Bennett (Posthumous)

As a forward air controller near Quang Tri, Republic of Vietnam, on June 29, 1972, Captain Bennett was the pilot of a light aircraft flying an artillery adjustment mission along a heavily defended segment of route structure.A large concentration of enemy troops was massing for an attack on a friendly unit. Captain Bennett requested tactical air support but was advised that none was available. He also requested artillery support but this too was denied due to the close proximity of friendly troops to the target. Captain Bennett was determined to aid the endangered unit and elected to strafe the hostile positions. After four such passes, the enemy force began to retreat. Captain Bennett continued the attack, but, as he completed his fifth strafing pass, his aircraft was struck by a surface-to-air missile, which severely damaged the left engine and the left main landing gear. As fire spread in the left engine, Captain Bennett realized that recovery at a friendly airfield was impossible. He instructed his observer to prepare for an ejection, but was informed by the observer that his parachute had been shredded by the force of the impacting missile. Although Captain Bennett had a good parachute, he knew that if he ejected, the observer would have no chance of survival. With complete disregard for his own life, Captain Bennett elected to ditch the aircraft into the Gulk of Tonkin, even though he realized that a pilot of this type aircraft had never survived a ditching. The ensuing impact upon the water caused the aircraft to cartwheel and severely damaged the front cockpit, making escape for Captain Bennett impossible. The observer successfully made his way out of the aircraft and was rescued. Captain Bennett's unparalleled concern for his companion, extraordinary heroism and intrepidity above and beyond the call of duty, at the cost of his life, were in keeping with the highest traditions of the military service and reflect great credit upon himself and the United States Air Force.

George E. Day

On 26 August 1967, Colonel (then Major) Day was forced to eject from his aircraft over North Vietnam when it was hit by ground fire. His right arm was broken in three places, and his left knee was badly sprained. He was immediately captured by hostile forces and taken to a prison camp where he was interrogated and severely tortured. After causing the guards to relax their vigilance, Colonel Day escaped into the jungle and began the trek toward South Vietnam. Despite injuries inflicted by fragments of a bomb or rocket, he continued southward surviving only on a few berries and uncooked frogs. He successfully evaded enemy patrols and reached the Ben Hai River, where he encountered United States artillery barrages. With the aid of a bamboo log float, Colonel Day swam across the river and entered the demilitarized zone. Due to delirium, he lost his sense of direction and wandered aimlessly for several days. After several unsuccessful attempts to signal United States aircraft, he was ambushed and recaptured by the Viet Cong, sustaining gunshot wounds to his left hand and thigh. He was returned to the prison from which he had escaped and later was moved to Hanoi after giving his captors false information to questions put before him. Physically, Colonel Day was totally debilitated and unable to perform even the simplest task for himself. Despite his many injuries, he continued to offer maximum resistance. His personal bravery in the face of deadly enemy pressure was significant in saving the lives of fellow aviators who were still flying against the enemy. Colonel Day's conspicuous gallantry and intrepidity at the risk of his life above and beyond the call of duty are in keeping with the highest traditions of the United States Air Force and reflect great credit upon himself and the Armed Forces of the United States.

Merlyn H. Dethlefsen

On March 10, 1967, Major Dethlefsen (then Captain) was one of a flight of F–105 aircraft engaged in a fire suppression mission designed to destroy a key antiaircraft defensive complex containing surface-to-air-missiles (SAM), an exceptionally heavy concentration of antiaircraft artillery, and other automatic weapons. The defensive network was situated to dominate the approach and provide protection to an important North Vietnam industrial center that was scheduled to be attacked by fighter bombers immediately after the strike by Major Dethlefsen's flight. In the initial attack on the defensive complex the lead aircraft was crippled, and Major Dethlefsen's aircraft was extensively damaged by the intense enemy fire. Realizing that the success of the impending fighter bomber attack on the center now depended on his ability to effectively suppress the defensive fire, Major Dethlefsen ignored the enemy's overwhelming firepower and the damage to his aircraft and pressed his attack. Despite a continuing hail of antiaircraft fire, deadly surface-to-air missiles, and counterattacks by MIG interceptors, Major Dethlefsen flew repeated close range strikes to silence the enemy defensive positions with bombs and cannon fire. His action in rendering ineffective the defensive SAM and antiaircraft artillery sites enabled the ensuing fighter bombers to strike successfully the important industrial target without loss or damage to their aircraft, thereby appreciably reducing the enemy's ability to provide essential war material. Major Dethlefsen's conspicuous gallantry, consummate skill and selfless dedication to this significant mission were in keeping with the highest traditions of the United States Air Force and reflect great credit upon himself and the Armed Forces of his country.

Bernard F. Fisher

For conspicuous gallantry and intrepidity at the risk of his life above and beyond the call of duty. On that date (10 March 1966), the special forces camp at A Shau was under attack by 2,000 North Vietnamese Army Regulars. Hostile troops had positioned themselves between the airstrip and the camp. Other hostile troops had surrounded the camp and were continuously raking it with automatic weapons fire from the surrounding hills. The tops of the 1,500-foot hills were obscured by an 800-foot ceiling, limiting aircraft maneuverability and forcing pilots to operate within range of hostile gun positions, which often were able to fire down on the attacking aircraft. During the battle, Major Fisher observed a fellow airman crash land on the battle-torn airstrip. In the belief that the downed pilot was seriously injured and in imminent danger of capture, Major Fisher announced his intention to land on the airstrip to effect a rescue. Although aware of the extreme danger and likely failure of such an attempt, he elected to continue. Directing his own air cover, he landed his aircraft and taxied almost the full length of the runway, which was littered with battle debris and parts of an exploded aircraft. While effecting a successful rescue of the downed pilot, heavy ground fire was observed, with nineteen bullets striking his aircraft. In the face of the withering ground fire, he applied power and gained enough speed to lift-off at the overrun of the airstrip. Major Fisher's conspicuous gallantry, his profound concern for his fellow airman, and his intrepidity at the risk of his life above and beyond the call of duty are in the highest traditions of the United States Air Forces and reflect great credit upon himself and the Armed Forces of his country.

James P. Fleming

For conspicuous gallantry and intrepidity in action at the risk of his life above and beyond the call of duty. On 26 November 1968, Captain Fleming (then First Lieutenant) distinguished himself as the Aircraft Commander of a UH–1F transport helicopter near Duc Co, Republic of Vietnam. On that date, Captain Fleming went to the aid of a six-man Special Forces Long Range Reconnaissance Patrol that was in danger of being overrun by a large, heavily armed hostile force. Despite the knowledge that one helicopter had been downed by intense hostile fire, Captain Fleming descended, and balanced his helicopter on a river bank with the tail boom hanging over open water. The patrol could not penetrate to the landing site and he was forced to withdraw. Dangerously low on fuel, Captain Fleming repeated his original landing maneuver. Disregarding his own safety, he remained in this exposed position. Hostile fire crashed through his windscreen as the patrol boarded his helicopter. Captain Fleming made a successful takeoff through a barrage of hostile fire and recovered safely at a forward base. Captain Fleming's conspicuous gallantry, his profound concern for his fellowmen, and his intrepidity at the risk of his life above and beyond the call of duty are in keeping with the highest traditions of the United States Air Force and reflect great credit upon himself and the Armed Forces of his country.

Joe M. Jackson

For conspicuous gallantry and intrepidity in action at the risk of his life above and beyond the call of duty. Colonel Jackson distinguished himself as pilot of a C–123 aircraft in the Republic of Vietnam, on 12 May 1968. On that date, Colonel Jackson volunteered to attempt the rescue of a three-man USAF Combat Control Team from the Special Forces Camp at Kham Duc. Hostile forces had overrun the forward outpost and established gun positions on the airstrip. They were raking the camp with small arms, mortars, light and heavy automatic weapons, and recoilless rifle fire. The camp was engulfed in flames and ammunition dumps were continuously exploding and littering the runway with debris. In addition, eight aircraft had been destroyed by the intense enemy fire and one aircraft remained on the runway reducing its usable length to only 2,200 feet. To further complicate the landing, the weather was deteriorating rapidly, thereby permitting only one airstrike prior to his landing. Although fully aware of the extreme danger and likely failure of such an attempt, Colonel Jackson elected to land his aircraft and attempt the rescue. Displaying superb airmanship and extraordinary heroism, he landed his aircraft near the point where the Combat Control Team was reported to be hiding. While on the ground, his aircraft was the target of intense hostile fire. A rocket landed in front of the nose of the aircraft but failed to explode. Once the Combat Control Team was aboard, Colonel Jackson succeeded in getting airborne despite the hostile fire directed across the runway in front of his aircraft. Colonel Jackson's conspicuous gallantry, his profound concern for his fellowman, and his intrepidity at risk of his life above and beyond the call of duty are in keeping with the highest traditions of the United States Air Force and reflect great credit upon himself, and the Armed Forces of his country.

William A. Jones III

For conspicuous gallantry and intrepidity in action at the risk of his life above and beyond the call of duty. On 1 September 1968, Colonel Jones distinguished himself as the pilot of an A–1H Skyraider aircraft near Dong Hoi, North Vietnam. On that day, as the on-scene commander in the attempted rescue of a downed United States pilot, Colonel Jones' aircraft was repeatedly hit by heavy and accurate antiaircraft fire. On one of his low passes, Colonel Jones felt an explosion beneath his aircraft and his cockpit rapidly filled with smoke. With complete disregard of the possibility that his aircraft might still be burning, he unhesitatingly continued his search for the downed pilot. On this pass, he sighted the survivor and a multiple-barrel gun position firing at him from near the top of a karst formation. He could not attack the gun position on that pass for fear he would endanger the downed pilot. Leaving himself exposed to the gun position, Colonel Jones attacked the position with cannon and rocket fire on two successive passes. On his second pass, the aircraft was hit with multiple rounds of automatic weapons fire. One round impacted the Yankee Extraction System rocket mounted directly behind the headrest, igniting the rocket. His aircraft was observed to burst into flames in the center fuselage section, with flames engulfing the cockpit area. He pulled the extraction handle, jettisoning the canopy. The influx of fresh air made the fire burn with greater intensity for a few moments, but since the rocket motor had already burned, the extraction system did not pull Colonel Jones from the aircraft. Despite searing pains from severe burns sustained on his arms, hands, neck, shoulders, and face, Colonel Jones pulled his aircraft into a climb and attempted to transmit the location of the downed pilot and the enemy gun position to the other aircraft in the area. His calls were blocked by other aircraft transmissions repeatedly directing him to bail out and within seconds his transmitters were disabled and he could receive only on one channel. Completely disregarding his injuries, he elected to fly his crippled aircraft back to his base and pass on essential information for the rescue rather than bail out. Colonel Jones successfully landed his heavily damaged aircraft and passed the information to a debriefing officer while on the operating table. As a result of his heroic actions and complete disregard for his personal safety, the downed pilot was rescued later in the day. Colonel Jones' conspicuous gallantry, his profound concern for his fellow man, and his intrepidity at the risk of his life, above and beyond the call of duty, are in keeping with the highest traditions of the United States Air Force and reflect great credit upon himself and the Armed Forces of his country.

John L. Levitow

For conspicuous gallantry and intrepidity in action at the risk of his life above and beyond the call of duty. Sergeant John L. Levitow (then Airman First Class), United States Air Force, distinguished himself by exceptional heroism on 24 February 1969, while assigned as a loadmaster aboard an AC–47 aircraft flying a night mission in support of Long Binh Army Post, Republic of Vietnam. On that date Sergeant Levitow's aircraft was struck by a hostile mortar round. The resulting explosion ripped a hole two feet in diameter through the wing and fragments made over 3,500 holes in the fuselage. All occupants of the cargo compartment were wounded and helplessly slammed against the floor and fuselage. The explosion tore an activated flare from the grasp of a crewmember who had been launching flares to provide illumination for Army ground troops engaged in combat. Sergeant Levitow, though stunned by the concussion of the blast and suffering from over forty fragment wounds in the back and legs, staggered to his feet and turned to assist the man nearest to him who had been knocked down and was bleeding heavily. As he was moving his wounded comrade forward and away from the opened cargo compartment door, he saw the smoking flare ahead of him in the aisle. Realizing the danger involved and completely disregarding his own wounds, Sergeant Levitow started toward the burning flare. The aircraft was partially out of control and the flare was rolling wildly from side to side. Sergeant Levitow struggled forward despite the loss of blood from his many wounds and the partial loss of feeling in his right leg. Unable to grasp the rolling flare with his hands, he threw himself bodily upon the burning flare. Hugging the deadly device to his body, he dragged himself back to the rear of the aircraft and hurled the flare through the open cargo door. At that instant the flare separated and ignited in the air, but clear of the aircraft. Sergeant Levitow, by his selfless and heroic actions, saved the aircraft and its entire crew from certain death and destruction. Sergeant Levitow's conspicuous gallantry, his profound concern for his fellowmen, and his intrepidity at the risk of his life above and beyond the call of duty are in keeping with the highest traditions of the United States Air Force and reflect great credit upon himself and the Armed Forces of his country.

Lance P. Sijan (Posthumous)

While on a flight over North Vietnam on 9 November 1967, Captain Sijan ejected from his disabled aircraft and successfully evaded capture for more than six weeks. During this time, he was seriously injured and suffered from shock and extreme weight loss due to lack of food. After being captured by North Vietnamese soldiers, Captain Sijan was taken to a holding point for subsequent transfer to a Prisoner of War camp. In his emaciated and crippled condition, he overpowered one of his guards and crawled into the jungle, only to be recaptured after several hours. He was then transferred to another prison camp where he was kept in solitary confinement and interrogated at length. During interrogation, he was severely tortured; however, he did not divulge any information to his captors. Captain Sijan lapsed into delirium and was placed in the care of another prisoner. During his intermittent periods of consciousness until his death, he never complained of his physical condition and, on several occasions, spoke of future escape attempts. Captain Sijan's extraordinary heroism and intrepidity above and beyond the call of duty at the cost of his life are in keeping with the highest traditions of the United States Air Force and reflect great credit upon himself and the Armed Forces of the United States.

Leo K. Thorsness

For conspicuous gallantry and intrepidity in action at the risk of his life above and beyond the call of duty. On 19 April 1967, as pilot of an F–105 aircraft, Lieutenant Colonel (then Major) Thorsness was on a surface-to-air missile suppression mission over North Vietnam. On that date, Lieutenant Colonel Thorsness and his wingman attacked and silenced a surface-to-air missile site with air-to-ground missiles, and then destroyed a second surface-to-air missile site with bombs. In the attack on the second missile site, Lieutenant Colonel Thorsness' wingman was shot down by intensive antiaircraft fire, and the two crew members abandoned their aircraft. Lieutenant Colonel Thorsness circled the descending parachutes to keep the crew members in sight and relay their position to the Search and Rescue Center. During this maneuver, a MIG–17 was sighted in the area. Lieutenant Colonel Thorsness immediately initiated an attack and destroyed the MIG. Because his aircraft was low on fuel, he was forced to depart the area in search of a tanker. Upon being advised that two helicopters were orbiting over the downed crew's position and that there were hostile MIGs in the area posing a serious threat to the helicopters, Lieutenant Colonel Thorsness, despite his low fuel condition, decided to return alone through a hostile environment of surface-to-air missile and antiaircraft defenses to the downed crew's position. As he approached the area, he spotted four MIG–17 aircraft and immediately initiated an attack on the MIGs, damaging one and driving the others away from the rescue scene. When it became apparent that an aircraft in the area was critically low on fuel and the crew would have to abandon the aircraft unless they could reach a tanker, Lieutenant Colonel Thorsness, although critically short on fuel himself, helped to avert further possible loss of life and a friendly aircraft by recovering at a forward operating base, thus allowing the aircraft in emergency fuel condition to refuel safely. Lieutenant Colonel Thorsness' extraordinary heroism, self-sacrifice, and personal bravery involving conspicuous risk of life were in the highest traditions of the military service, and have reflected great credit upon himself and the United States Air Force.

Hilliard A. Wilbanks (Posthumous)

For conspicuous gallantry and intrepidity in action at the risk of his life above and beyond the call of duty. As a forward air controller near Dalat, Republic of Vietnam, on 24 February 1967, Captain Wilbanks was pilot of an unarmed, light aircraft flying visual reconnaissance ahead of a South Vietnam Army Ranger Battalion. His intensive search revealed a well-concealed and numerically superior hostile force poised to ambush the advancing Rangers. The Viet Cong, realizing that Captain Wilbank's discovery had compromised their position and ability to launch a surprise attack, immediately fired on the small aircraft with all available fire power. The enemy then began advancing against the exposed forward elements of the Ranger force which were pinned down by devastating fire. Captain Wilbanks recognized that close support aircraft could not arrive in time to enable the Rangers to withstand the advancing enemy onslaught. With full knowledge of the limitations of his unarmed, unarmored, light reconnaissance aircraft, and the great danger imposed by the enemy's vast fire power, he unhesitatingly assumed a covering, close support role. Flying through a hail of withering fire at treetop level, Captain Wilbanks passed directly over the advancing enemy and inflicted many casualties by firing his rifle out of the side window of his aircraft. Despite increasingly intense antiaircraft fire, Captain Wilbanks continued to completely disregard his own safety and made repeated low passes over the enemy to divert their fire away from the Rangers. His daring tactics successfully interrupted the enemy advance, allowing the Rangers to withdraw to safety from their perilous position. During his final courageous attack to protect the withdrawing forces, Captain Wilbanks was mortally wounded and his bullet-riddled aircraft crashed between the opposing forces. Captain Wilbanks' magnificent action saved numerous friendly personnel from certain injury or death. His unparalleled concern for his fellowman and his extraordinary heroism were in the highest traditions of the military service, and have reflected great credit upon himself and the United States Air Force.

Gerald O. Young

For conspicuous gallantry and intrepidity at the risk of his life above and beyond the call of duty. Captain Young distinguished himself on 9 November 1967 while serving as a Helicopter Rescue Crew Commander in Southeast Asia. Captain Young was flying escort for another helicopter attempting the night rescue of an Army ground reconnaissance team in imminent danger of death or capture. Previous attempts had resulted in the loss of two helicopters to hostile ground fire. The endangered team was positioned on the side of a steep slope which required unusual airmanship on the part of Captain Young to effect pickup. Heavy automatic weapons fire from the surrounding enemy severely damaged one rescue helicopter, but it was able to extract three of the team. The commander of this aircraft recommended to Captain Young that further rescue attempts be abandoned because it was not possible to suppress the concentrated fire from enemy automatic weapons. With full knowledge of the danger involved, and the fact that supporting helicopter gunships were low on fuel and ordnance, Captain Young hovered under intense fire until the remaining survivors were aboard. As he maneuvered the aircraft for takeoff, the enemy appeared at point-blank range and raked the aircraft with automatic weapons fire. The aircraft crashed, inverted, and burst into flames. Captain Young escaped through a window of the burning aircraft. Disregarding serious burns, Captain Young aided one of the wounded men and attempted to lead the hostile forces away from his position. Later, despite intense pain from his burns, he declined to accept rescue because he had observed hostile forces setting up automatic weapons positions to entrap any rescue aircraft. For more than 17 hours he evaded the enemy until rescue aircraft could be brought into the area. Through his extraordinary heroism, aggressiveness, and concern for his fellowman, Captain Young reflected the highest credit upon himself, the United States Air Force, and the Armed Forces of his country.

Appendix D. Glossary

Ace—Combat pilot credited with five or more victories over enemy aircraft.

Afterburner—An auxiliary combustion chamber in the aft section of a jet engine where the unused oxygen of exhaust gases is used to burn a second fuel spray resulting in increased thrust.

Aileron—A control surface on the wing, used to control the rolling movements of the airplane.

Air Defense Command or Aerospace Defense Command—A major air command of the USAF, responsible for providing air defense of the US.

Antiaircraft artillery (AAA)—Projectile weapons with their related equipment, as searchlights, radar, etc., employed on the ground or on ships to strike at airborne aircraft.

Autorotation—The free rotation of rotor blades without engine power; the unpowered descent of a helicopter.

Aviation cadet—A person in training to become a commissioned AF officer with an aeronautical rating.

Bailout—An escape from an aircraft by parachuting.

Bear—Nickname for the backseat electronic warfare officer in certain USAF fighter airplaines.

Ceiling—The maximum height at which an airplane or aircrew can fly; the height of the lower surface of a cloud layer.

Close air support—Air support provided to friendly surface forces, consisting of air attacks with guns, bombs, guided airborne missiles or rockets on hostile surface forces, their installations or vehicles so close to surface operations as to require detailed coordination between air and friendly forces.

Cluster bombs—Many small bombs carried in a single container or dispenser.

Counterinsurgency—Operations against a nonregular or guerrilla force.

Defense suppression—Military operations to neutralize or destroy the enemy's defensive systems.

Ditch—To force-land an aircraft on water with the intention of abandonment.

Ejection seat—A seat designed to catapult a flyer from an airplane.

Endurance (aircraft)—The aircraft's ability to remain airborne without in-flight refueling.

Escort—Airplane(s) flying to provide protection for other aircraft.

Feet wet—Pilot radio terminology which means he is heading toward or flying over open water.

Final approach—The last leg of a landing pattern, during which the aircraft is lined up with the runway and is held to a fairly constant speed and rate of descent.

Flak—Explosive projectiles fired from antiaircraft guns.

Flaps—Control surfaces often found on the trailing edge of a wing which increase the lift or drag of an airplane.

Flareship—Aircraft which dispenses illuminating flares for night operations.

Flight leader—A pilot in command of a flight of aircraft.

Forward air controller (FAC)—A pilot responsible for directing aircraft to targets by radio in a close-air-support operation.

Ground controlled approach (GCA)—An instrument approach for landing in response to radio directions from a controller observing the aircraft on a radar set.

Groundfire—Fire, such as antiaircraft fire, that emanates from the ground.

Gunships—Helicopters or cargo aircraft modified with guns for a ground attack role.

Ho Chi Minh Trail—Supply route from North Vietnam through Laos to South Vietnam. Named after famous North Vietnamese leader.

Insurgency—Nonregular movement against the established government.

Jettison—To throw out or drop, especially in an emergency situation, cargo, bombs, fuel, or armament to lighten or streamline the aircraft.

Jink—To jerk an aircraft about in evasive action.

Magazine—A structure or compartment for storing ammunition or explosives.

MIG—A popular designation for certain Russian fighter aircraft designed and developed by Mikoyan and Gurevich.

Oak leaf cluster—One cluster is worn for each subsequent award of the medal after the first.

Order of precedence (of Air Force medals)—Medal of Honor, Air Force Cross, Silver Star, Distinguished Flying Cross, Air Medal, Purple Heart.

Ordnance—Military weapons, ammunition, explosives, combat vehicles and battle materiel.

Pallet—A platform or shallow open box for holding supplies or materials for convenient storage or handling.

Paramedic—A medical technician qualified to participate in parachute activities, especially those involving rescue.

Pierced steel planking (PSP)—Metal strips pierced with numerous holes, used as a temporary surface for an airstrip.

Reconnaissance—Observation of an area to secure information about the terrain, or the weather, or the enemy and his installations.

Red River—Large North Vietnamese river which flows southeast through Hanoi to the Gulf of Tonkin.

Rocket pod—A container carrying rocket ammunition usually mounted on a wingtip or under a wing.

SAM—Surface-to-air missile.

Scramble—To launch aircraft as rapidly as possible. Airplanes and pilots on alert status are ready for the scramble order.

Shrike—Air-to-ground missile that locks on and guides toward a radar signal.

Sortie—A single mission flown in an aircraft.

Strafe—To fire an aircraft gun, usually at a ground target.

Strategic Air Command—A major air command of the USAF charged with carrying out strategic air operations.

Tanker aircraft—An aircraft used to refuel others in flight.

Trim—To adjust or balance an aircraft so that it maintains coordinated, balanced flight.

Turns (aircraft)—180-degree turn—maneuvering an aircraft to reverse course and head in the opposite direction.

Vietcong (VC)—Communist guerrillas who fought against the government of South Vietnam.

White phosphorous (Willie Pete)—A nonmetallic element that burns readily giving off thick, white smoke. Often used in target marking rockets or smoke grenades.

Wild weasel—Fighter aircraft designed to seek out and destroy enemy defenses.

Wingman—A pilot who flies his aircraft in formation with the flight leader's aircraft.

INDEX

☆ U.S. GOVERNMENT PRINTING OFFICE : 1985 O - 486-885